LONGTON

Longton

in the
Nineteenth Century

MARJORIE SEARSON

Copyright © Marjorie Searson, 2004

Published by Carnegie Publishing Ltd
Carnegie House
Chatsworth Road
Lancaster
LAI 4SL
www.carnegiepublishing.com

Copyright © Marjorie Searson, 2004

British Library Cataloguing-in-Publication data
A CIP record for this book is available from the British Library

ISBN 1-85936-124-2

Typeset in Adobe Garamond by Carnegie Publishing
Printed and bound in the UK by The Cromwell Press, Trowbridge, Wilts

Contents

For John

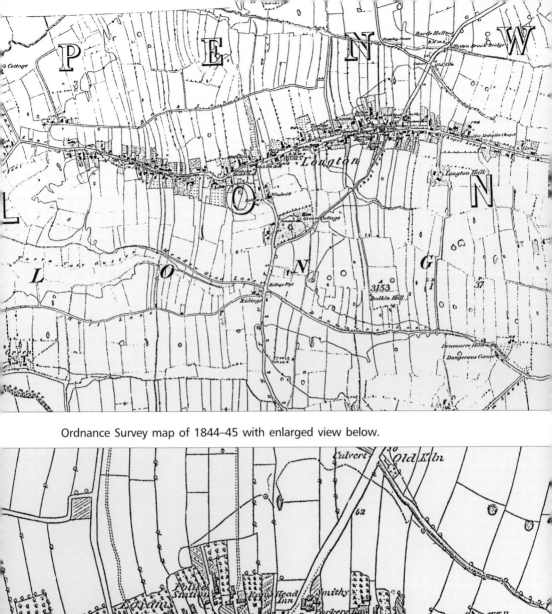

Ordnance Survey map of 1844–45 with enlarged view below.

Ordnance Survey map of 1894 with enlarged view below.

Extract from Ordnance Survey 25″ plans, Lancashire Sheets 68–7 and 68–9 (1911 edition), enlarged view below.

OS Map 1:20,560 scale 1967, with an enlarged view below.

Introduction

*M*Y FIRST BOOK, *Longton, a Village History,* was published in 1988. It was by its nature a concise, overall account of the growth of the village from prehistoric times to the present day.

I had filed away the notes and material I had collected, but was conscious that much of it concerned the nineteenth century which had not been explored in depth. Prior to 1800, the source material was limited, consisting of wills and inventories, a few parish records and evidence from similar research elsewhere. In contrast, after 1800, the amount of evidence is enormous – the decennial censuses, parish registers and magazines, the Tithe Map and the Ordnance Survey, trade directories, local newspapers and a wealth of authoritative material both national and regional. Above all, this evidence is, in most cases, accurate and reliable. To any historian this is intriguing, but it is also a challenge to add a new dimension to the history of where one lives. So out came the files, and the research began again.

The censuses of 1851 and 1881 were my starting point. The very first census had been made in 1801, in response to increased pressure on Parliament in 1800 to find out just how many people lived in Great Britain. Similar investigations had already been made in Holland, Spain and the United States, and detailed studies of

English society by Gregory King in 1688 and of the population of Aix-en-Provence in 1695. The need for reliable information had been urged in Parliament, even in 1753, but in the years that followed, a bitter debate as to whether the population was increasing or decreasing raged on, until the publication of Malthus's *Essay on the Principle of Population* in 1798. His treatise, which propounded that a population increase inevitably brought poverty, and published at a time of considerable social distress, made it essential for Parliament to take positive action.

The results of the 1801 census, which revealed a population of over nine million, was a surprise to a great many, and concern grew by 1811 when the figure reached over ten million, particularly when it was found that the greatest increase was in the North and Midland counties whose major towns were growing out of all proportion to the traditional centres of population. John Rickman, who had been instrumental in carrying out the 1801 census, had proved his point that, if Malthus was right, then social improvements, if they were to be effective, had to be based on accurate statistics.[1]

Between 1801 and 1831 Rickman employed the overseer of the poor in each parish 'or other fit person' to complete the required forms. These were not so detailed as later censuses were to become, and only listed the households and their occupants, divided into sex and occupation. The results were sent to the Clerk of the Peace and then to the Government's Home Department. Although basic, the returns were honestly made and at the least indicated population trends region by region.

In 1837, a new Government department, the General Register office, had been created, headed by the Registrar General, whose duty was to register all live births. So when the 1841 Census was made, it fell to the Registrar General to adminsiter its collection through his network of superintendents and local registrars. Local registrars divided their areas into enumeration districts, some 30,000 in all, and thus it was possible to list everyone in a single day and so reduce the likelihood of errors or double entries. The blank forms were delivered to each household some days before the census date and when collected their details were transcribed by the enumerators into their own books which were then sent to the local registrar. Here they were checked with the superintendent and subsequently sent to London where a host of clerks, working in many cases twelve hours a day for several months, had the task of tabulating the findings.

So successful was the 1841 procedure that it was used in 1851 and subsequently until 1911 when punched cards were used for the later analysis. One or two improvements were however introduced to the questions asked. In 1851 exact places of birth and age were required together with marital state and relationship to the head of the household. It is these improvements which make the 1851 census the most useful from the historian's point of view.

The original household schedules for the censuses of 1841 to 1901 were destroyed in 1904, and what remain are the enumerators' books. Because these books are copies, made on occasions by

Extract from the Census of 1851.

Longton Hall Farm, off Chapel Lane. A c.16th-century house, extended in 1662 by William Walion and his wife who was possibly named Isabel. He was the local bailiff for the Shireburns of Stonyhurst who opened land in Longton at this time.

people who unwittingly may not have fully understood their instructions, some allowances have to be made. Errors were made in recording, and on occasions enumerators had to help because householders did not understand how to complete the schedules. Some could not remember where they were born or how old their children were, and women were sometimes unwilling to reveal their age or occasionally whether they had had an illegitimate child. The jobs which people did often proved difficult to describe accurately, and some magnified their importance, or as in the case of farmers, did not say how many acres they farmed or how many men they employed. Because of the detailed personal information contained in censuses, a hundred years have to elapse before they are available for public research.[2, 3]

However hesitant Parliament had been in 1800 to pass the 'Act for taking an Account of the Population of Great Britain, and the Increase or Diminution thereof', it could not have anticipated the wealth of information which it subsequently provided for historians and genealogists in future generations.

Likewise, when the Tithe Commutation Act was passed in 1836, it too provided later researchers with information which was invaluable for the study of land tenure and agricultural practices; without it, our knowledge of land use in Victorian England would be immeasurably poorer. The tithe was levied on all tenant farmers, being one tenth of the profits from the soil, farm stock or from personal earnings. The proceeds of this levy were paid to support the parish church, and when payments were made in kind, as in the case of cereals, these were stored in the local tithe barn. The payment of tithes had been bitterly resented for centuries, not only by non-conformists on religious grounds, but by the whole farming community. Why should the local parson receive such payments, won by hard back-breaking toil, they argued, when he contributed so little in return? Attempts to avoid payment were commonplace.

> We've cheated the parson,
> We'll cheat him again,
> For why should the vicar have one in ten?

The Tithe Act ended these payments in kind, replacing them with a rent charge on the land itself. It was not until 1891, however, that this rent was made payable by the landowner rather than the tenant, and 1936 before all tithes were finally extinguished and replaced by redemption annuities payable to the Crown for sixty years.

The 1836 Act appointed Tithe Commissioners who were charged 'to enable parties to identify the lands which are respectively subject to the several accounts of rent charge'.[4] To do so, each Tithe Award or Schedule was accompanied by a detailed map, and the two documents taken together show not only where each field, cottage, road and track was, but who owned and tenanted the land and what crops were being grown at the time. The Longton map of 1838 is some eighteen feet long and to a scale of about twenty-five inches to the mile. Its accompanying schedule is equally cumbersome. It shows that the tithes were paid partly to the lay 'impropriator' Colonel Rawstorne and partly to the curate of Penwortham.

The Longton map can be used in conjunction with the later Ordnance Survey map of the village, dating from 1848. Earlier maps, such as Christopher Saxton's of 1577 and William Yates' of 1786 show a village growing and developing over the centuries, but the first Ordnance Survey was far superior in detail and accuracy to anything previously produced. Taking these two maps together with the 1851 census, even allowing for the time-scale between each, makes it possible to plot houses, roads and tracks, and make informed 'guesses' about who lived where in mid-Victorian Longton.

Trade directories also reveal a good deal about the village, and because they were produced regularly they list the principal local farmers, tradesmen, shopkeepers and local 'worthies'. They add to one's existing knowledge, although it has to be remembered that, as trade publications, those listed paid to have their names entered and therefore not everyone would necessarily be included.

Sadly, wills and their accompanying inventories, which are invaluable for the study of social life in the seventeenth and early eighteenth centuries, are of little use to the historian. The requirement to produce an inventory of the goods and chattels of the deceased lapsed after the mid-1750s.

Nineteenth-century parish registers and Quarter Sessions reports are also more useful to the genealogist than the historian. After the Poor Law Amendment Act of 1834, the removal and affiliation orders enacted at Quarter Sessions disappear, and their transactions become less informative, although Overseers of the Poor accounts and workhouse records remain a fascinating if sad reminder of the old Poor Law as it affected the local poor and destitute. With all this information at hand, it is therefore understandable that any local historian needs little encouragement to reconstruct his or her village in the nineteenth century.

CHAPTER ONE

Before 1800: A Golden Age?

THE YEAR 1800 is a convenient date to begin. It saw the end of an era which many regarded as a golden age. A time of leisure and elegance which George Eliot invoked in *Adam Bede*, when a man might 'live chiefly in the country, among pleasant seats and homesteads' and when 'Life was not a task to him, but a sinecure'.[5] Yet there was another England, already visible to George Eliot, when 'Leisure is gone, gone where the spinning wheels are gone and the pack-horses, and the slow waggons and the pedlars, who brought bargains to the door on sunny afternoons'.

Many regarded 1800 as a watershed. Before was a pastoral England, dominated by agriculture, a world which was never to return. After came disturbance, insurrection and the rise of an urban-dominated economy. This division may be simplistic, for this golden age did not end in 1799 nor did the Industrial Revolution begin in 1800; change came gradually. Nevertheless 1800 can for our purpose be the watershed between one era and the next.

From the 1740s Britain's population had increased steadily from seven and three-quarter million to well over ten million by 1801. The population of London in 1801 was almost a million and Lancashire, with nearly 700,000, was the third most populous county, after Yorkshire and Middlesex. Towns such as Bristol and Norwich, which had been major cities, were being rapidly overtaken by Manchester, Liverpool, Leeds and Birmingham. Despite this, over five and a half million people in 1801 still lived in rural areas.

A period of low prices and steady incomes in the first half of the century enabled those with a surplus to improve their living standards, thus stimulating the economy and the growth of manufacturing. More plentiful food supplies probably had an effect on the population making it more healthy and less prone to disease. The steady rise in population from the 1740s further boosted the economy.[6]

Yet England in the late eighteenth century was a country of great inequalities, not only in living standards, but in power and prestige.

At the top of the social pyramid was the landed aristocracy, small in the number but vastly wealthy and politically powerful. Below them was the gentry, the squire who wielded considerable power and influence at local level, and some of the clergy who lived well on their church land and the income from the payment of tithes. Beneath them were the freeholders and substantial tenant farmers whose fortunes varied considerably. The smaller landowners had little to invest in improved methods of agriculture, and as a result they found life a struggle. On the other hand, the tenant farmer with a large holding did well and his lifestyle visibly improved.

These groups increasingly required the services and expertise of a growing middle class – lawyers, surveyors, brokers, master crafts-men and merchants, and they too, having benefitted from the fees and prices they could charge, sought to rise up the social scale. They in turn bought land for 'the ultimate proof of success in business was the ability to leave it'.[7]

At the bottom of the social scale were the artisans, labourers and the poor. They were a very mixed group. Artisans, having served their apprenticeships, might in turn become craftsmen and look forward to a reasonably comfortable way of life. But for labourers, servants and the poor, keeping body and soul together was an endless struggle. By 1750 half the working population were wage-earners and consisted of farm workers, weavers, spinners and domestic servants. The rest were self-employed – thatchers, tinkers, pedlars and the like. All were dependent one way or another on the vagaries of the economic situation and the weather. Many were able to supplement their earnings by owning a loom, but they too were still heavily dependent on market forces. The under-employed joined the sick, the elderly, the disabled and young children in an under-class which was increasingly dependent upon poor relief. In 1800, 28% of the population received such relief, administered as it had been since 1662 by the parish. Parish ratepayers thought that the poor were basically feckless, had brought most of their problems upon themselves, and given any spare cash would spend it on drink. The poor on the other hand had a statutory right to the dole in their parish of 'settlement' and at least the parish overseers could be sympathetic when they knew the paupers' background. Nevertheless there were instances of appalling insensitivity, especially where pregnant women sought help, for no parish wanted to be saddled with a pauper bastard. By the early 1800s the problem of pauperism had reached astron-omic proportions requiring national rather than local hand-to-mouth expedients.

Although for one in five families daily life was one of unremitting toil with the ever-present fear of the poverty trap, for the rest of the working population the half-century up to 1800 had its compensations.

The family was all-important. But contrary to popular belief, the extended family was not the norm. In fact, the family consisted of husband and wife and their young children. Older children left to go into apprenticeships or into domestic service in their early teens. In-laws, if they were still alive – and many were not – did not live with their married children. As local smallholders had to work cooperatively, agreeing the crops to be grown in the open fields, and sharing ploughs and horses, so in family life every member had his or her duties from an early age. Young children were expected to help in and around the smallholding or at the spinning wheel, and few of the elderly retired, unless forced to do so by ill-health or infirmity. Marriage and starting a family was delayed until the young couple had somewhere to live. So the age of marriage was late, and many never lived to see their children grow up to adulthood. Restraint was exercised in limiting the size of the family, for too many young mouths to feed could easily lead to pauperism. Illegitimacy was low, for the moral strictures of the local community were strong.

People were used to discipline and submission. Young children were expected to be obedient and frequently experienced physical punishment if they disobeyed. Women had no rights to matrimonial property – 'In marriage husband and wife are one person, and that person is the husband'.[8] Among the affluent, making a good marriage was essential, and once married a lady must obey her husband, give him an heir to the estate, and see to the running of the household and the control of the servants. Women were not expected to voice an opinion, but to be virtuous and docile and exhibit the feminine social graces.

For the ordinary woman, despite its legal restrictions marriage offered security, and a status of sorts in the local community. Life which revolved round the farm, domestic industry or business demanded and got a working partnership between husband and wife. Occasionally women did attain independence. Unmarried daughters and widows often kept on the family business after their father's or husband's death, at a time when women tended to outlive men anyway.

Everyday life revolved around the seasons on the one hand, and holy days on the other, from sheep-shearing to rush-bearing and the harvest festival. Christmas, Easter and Whitsun were occasions

Longton church, 1773–1886.

for enjoyment, interwoven with earlier pagan rituals such as wassailing and 'pace-egging'. Ordinary men and women adjusted their lives, not only to the necessity of earning a living, looking after their families and coping with occasional crises, but also to living within the community, be it town or village, where customs established by tradition governed the fabric of day-to-day life.

Although 1800 was a watershed, the seeds of change were clearly sown long before. It seemed as if England, aware of its future as 'the workshop of the world', was alive with activity. The low prices and steady incomes already mentioned, provided a stimulus to the market economy. Those with money or skills to invest, coupled with ambition, a competitive spirit and, in some cases, a degree of luck, found success. After the establishment of the Bank of England in 1694, confidence in the money market had grown steadily. City banks issued notes and gradually bills of exchange and the use of credit became commonplace. Credit enabled business to expand and provided finance for projects such as turnpikes, canals, land improvement and trading speculations.

But central to England's growth was its successful overseas trading position. Raw materials from the colonies, the West Indies, Canada and India were imported without let or hindrance, due to the Navigation Acts which gave the British merchant fleet a monopoly of the carrying trade. The number of merchants and middlemen expanded to meet the ever-growing demand at home for foreign goods, and for the re-export of luxury goods to the European markets. This enormous increase in demand for goods of all description in turn stimulated the need for improvements in transportation and in more efficient means of production.

Even before the era of canal construction, rivers were deepened and made navigable, thus opening up trade with many inland towns. Improved roads were also essential, for packhorses were the only method of carrying goods any distance, and a journey up the Great North Road from London to Edinburgh, even in 1740, could take two weeks. The establishment of turnpike trusts eventually linked London to the major cities, and although they were not cheap to use, they greatly reduced the journey time. Turnpikes gave rise to stagecoach services, with their attendant hostels and inns, and later in the century, to civil engineering improvements in road servicing and bridge-building.

The manufacture of goods also required greater efficiency. Still dominated by guild regulations, most industries were on a small scale and heavily dependent on workers employed in their cottages or small workshops. Industry was highly labour-intensive and many processes were carried out by a vast network of sub-contractors. Manufacturers were not yet ready to envisage revolutionary inventions, but improved their existing technology, and used their existing labour force more effectively, recruiting more when demand was at its height. By 1715 the Darbys of Coalbrookdale were pioneers in developing the use of coke for iron smelting, but they kept their innovation secret. Newcomen's steam engine, perfected in 1712, was principally confined to pumping water from mineshafts, and John Kay's flying shuttle of 1733 was regarded with suspicion. Protectionism held sway and early revolutionary ideas were regarded as a threat to the status quo. The South Sea Bubble of 1720 had been a salutary warning to many investors, and as a result most industrial investment was limited to the input of private capital.

In agriculture the pressure for change was also inevitable, but it too came but slowly. Lord Townshend on his Norfolk estates, and Robert Bakewell, a Leicestershire farmer, had been early pioneers in the introduction of turnips, better crop rotation and improved sheep and cattle breeding. But in middle England, from Dorset in the south west to Yorkshire in the north east, was a huge swathe of countryside which was still cultivated under the uneconomic and wasteful open-field system. Here small farmers had little capital for enclosure, and agricultural labourers who stood to lose their rights of common were resistant to change. Nevertheless the great landowners and large tenant farmers, recognising the benefits of better stock and heavier crops, and of course increased profits, pressed ahead with private enclosure acts or enclosure by local agreement. Inevitably those who resisted were those who suffered the consequences. Many smallholders were forced to sell up and leave, and cottagers and squatters on the common or waste lands were summarily evicted, with little alternative but to join the ranks of the paupers, dependent on poor-law handouts from the parishes. Enclosure changed the landscape of England. Gone were the open fields of the central and southern counties, replaced by hedged fields and wide straight roads. Many cottagers, if not reduced to pauperism, became day labourers plying for hire under a new capitalism which had abolished the age-old customary relationship which had existed between lord and tenant.

Yet despite the hardship which enclosure undoubtedly caused for many thousands of rural working class people, the one redeeming feature was that England, despite its rising population, was able to feed itself as a nation.

And feed themselves many did. Economic buoyancy gave many spare cash, which was used primarily for more food and in provisions such as tea, coffee and sugar which had previously been thought of as luxuries. For the well-to-do, meals were gargantuan affairs, liberally washed down with wine, punch and strong beer. Alcohol was drunk in large quantities in all walks of life and some 50,000 inns and hostelries were reported to exist in the middle years of the century. But the poor did not enjoy these material improvements, living as they did on a monotonous diet of mainly bread and cheese, with a little fat bacon on occasions.

It was an age of spending rather then saving. With the increased circulation of newspapers and magazines, the advertising of new and tempting goods made it essential for those who could afford it to keep up with the Joneses, and buy the latest in furniture, fabrics, tableware and the like. Provincial town-dwellers were anxious to prove themselves as fashionable as those in London. For businessmen, this urge to spend brought them increased trade and increased profits, and few heeded the critics who deprecated society's materialism.

Georgian England has often been depicted as a golden age of 'solid, stable rural England', but immense political power was wielded by an oligarchy of the rich and powerful, who used their patronage and manipulative influence at all levels of society.

Each English county was represented by two members of Parliament and only freeholders worth 40s. a year were allowed to vote. There was no secret ballot and threats and bribes were widespread at election time. Once an MP was elected, pensions, positions

and sinecures were in his gift. The size and nature of the consti-
tuency bore no relation to its population, and democracy – as we
know it – was non existent. Authority was the prerequisite of the
rich, and the poor had no say in the matter. Local government
remained much as it had been under Elizabeth I. At parish level, it
was administered by local unpaid officials – the churchwardens,
overseers of the poor, highway surveyors and constables. These were
controlled by justices of the peace, usually the local squires.
Wielding extremely wide powers, JPs controlled not only parish
officials, but meted out summary justice to petty offenders and
committed more serious crimes to the Quarter Sessions. As the
century wore on, there was a growing undercurrent of crime,
disturbance and poverty, which could no longer be controlled on
a local piecemeal basis. Highwaymen, smugglers and local rioters
took the law into their own hands. Denied the franchise, the public
at large aired its grievances through newspapers, posters, cartoons
and pamphlets but such riots as there were, concerning food prices,
turnpike gates, wages or unpopular politicians, although violent,
were short-lived.

Despite the materialism and brutality of the age, the eighteenth
century was one of improved literacy, largely through the establishment of charity schools. With the desire to read, an ever-growing
number of books, magazines, newspapers, chapbooks and picture
books became readily available. Playhouses opened, even in
provincial towns. Handel and J C Bach settled in England and John
Gay's 'Beggars' Opera' was popular. Hogarth, Gainsborough and
Joshua Reynolds were employed by the nobility, where formerly
foreign painters had been commissioned. Chippendale, Sheraton
and the Adams brothers provided beautiful furniture and interior
decorations. All these gave taste and elegance to an age which still
had its bucolic side.

But in the later years of the century, the acquisitiveness and
materialism of society became tempered, not only by some critics

at home, but more significantly by events overseas. The war of American Independence and the American colonists' demands for 'no taxation without representation' struck a chord among English radicals. The French Revolution created a wave of fear in the Government, and Pitt passed series of acts to guard against sedition and unlawful meetings. These fears were very real, for a flood of radical literature such as Thomas Paine's *Rights of Man* (1791) had created a subtle change in the climate of opinion, which had been largely unspoken since the Cromwellian Revolution 150 years before. As it turned out, political consciousness was not yet formalised. In 1793 the war against France and the threat of invasion put patriotism before radicalism. Yet the seeds were sown. After the end of the war in 1815, with increased industrialisation, the inequalities between the haves and have-nots could no longer be denied.

CHAPTER TWO

Evolution or Revolution?

$\mathcal{T}$HE INDUSTRIAL REVOLUTION, a phrase coined by Arnold
Toynbee in 1881, was no sudden phenomenon. W. W.
Rostow[9] sees the period from 1783 to 1802 as the 'take-off' years
of Britain's economic development, followed by her 'drive to
maturity' in the years between 1802 and 1850. The inventions of
John Kay's flying shuttle, Hargreaves' spinning jenny, Crompton's
mule and Arkwright's water frame had slowly reformed the textile
industry, and Newcomen's steam pump and James Watts' steam
engine had revolutionised the coal, iron and engineering industries
and concentrated production in the North and Midlands. By 1850
technical progress had reached the stage whereby on the one hand,
huge iron castings could be forged and on the other machine tools
made for delicate precision work. In the textile industry the factory
system had completely transformed what had been a handicraft
occupation carried on at home, to a highly organised large-scale
production process – machine driven and employing thousands
of workers.

The factory system ushered in a totally new way of life which
for most Victorians was bewildering. It was a completely new
social experience for which few were equipped, but in a generation
it forced them to adopt new working methods, to move to a new
town in many cases, and also to face the vagaries of an economic

system which could leave them unemployed. For those not directly affected, it was hard to comprehend the social effects or to understand the upheaval which was created for thousands of men, women and children, abruptly forcing them into an entirely new existence.

Therefore reactions to the Industrial Revolution depended above all on one's position and attitude. For some it was an opportunity to accumulate wealth and to argue that by so doing, they were providing their operatives with daily bread. For those directly affected it meant 'the people must work – men, women and children are yoked together with iron and steam'. [10]

Nevertheless, up to 1850, Britain's economy was dependent upon basic industries. The production of consumer goods and services came later and it must be remembered that, despite all that has been written about the Industrial Revolution, in the 1851 census, 900,000 people in the UK – 20% – were employed in agriculture, and the country was self-supporting in food, at least when the harvest was good, despite the ever-increasing population. Life in the country went on very much as it had always done.

The effects of industrialisation on the tradition of handloom weaving and the continuance of agriculture, especially in areas like Longton, will be examined in more detail later.

One of the significant features of early Victorian Britain was the rapid increase in its population. One of the principal reasons for the first census of population taken in 1801 was to establish just how many people lived in Britain, and the figure of 10.6 million was greeted with disbelief. By 1841 it had risen to 16 million and 18 million by 1851. The basic reason for this was the coincidence of a fall in the death rate and the maintenance of a high birth rate. But it is simplistic to say that the improvement in preventive medicine was the main reason. Undoubtedly, deaths in childbirth and from smallpox, scurvy and other diseases were reduced, but infant mortality, especially in the late 1840s, remained

high. It was suggested[11] that a couple would need to produce five
or six children in order to ensure that two would grow to ultimate
maturity. At the same time, the economic uncertainties of the first
half of the nineteenth century did have an effect, particularly on
marriage. Many delayed marriage until they were able to support
a family, and more significantly many young people of both sexes
remained single. These factors must be taken together, and will
be looked at in more detail later in regard to Longton. But the
fact remains that people were living longer and more babies were
being born. The census also showed a very young population. In
1841 45% of the population of Britain was under the age of twenty
and only 7% were over sixty years of age.

This was a pattern very similar to pre-industrial society,
indicating that people in the early Victorian age had not yet come
to terms with life in an industrial age. The essential difference
can be seen in our own age, where the number of young people
is reduced, but the number of older people is increased, thus
changing the social pyramid, and inevitably posing problems for
government, when a small proportion of young people have to
meet the demands of an ageing population.

Although, as we have seen, over 20% of the population of the
UK in 1851 was employed in agriculture, and many more worked
in related trades, such as rural craftsmen and small shopkeepers
in village communities, for the first time in the country's history,
over half its people lived in towns. Some of this was due to the
increase of births over deaths in the newly developing towns, but
also to immigration from the surrounding rural areas. This shift
was a matter of considerable concern to early Victorian statesmen.
A hint of the political repercussions was evident by 1800, as we
saw in Chapter One, but the social implications became more
apparent and more alarming as the century wore on. The Reverend
Thomas Malthus, writing in his *Essay on the Principle of Population*
in 1798, had a profound effect upon the political and economic

thinking of the age. He had stated that population had a tendency to grow faster than the means of feeding itself. But he also said that in practice population would prevent this from happening by 'positive and preventive' checks. Positive checks he cited as extreme poverty, poor care of children, harsh working conditions and bad weather and diseases, which were all beyond the control of the individual. Preventive checks, he regarded as contraceptives and 'moral restraints', and thereby he presented people with the need to make positive personal choice of lifestyle. 'Whatever other remedies may be prescribed, therefore, restrictions upon the marriages of the poor are an indispensable part of the regime to be observed.' It is hard for us to imagine the genuine fears that many Victorians had, faced with the ever-increasing population and ever-mindful of Malthus, and the consequent threat posed to their established way of life. Many regarded the old rural existence as the norm and the new towns as problems which required solution. They had difficulty in realising that towns and cities had grown up and were permanent features of the industrial age, and that the unprecedented increase in the population affected not only urban areas, but were problems in the countryside as well.

Malthus had regarded it as necessary for the poor to exercise moral restraint and Arthur Young (1771) in his *A Tour through the East of England* had written that they 'must be kept poor or they will never be industrious'. For centuries the poor had not necessarily been regarded as needy, but as that section of society which used its hands to earn its wages, and which might, for one reason or another, become paupers, and therefore a liability. But the decennial census figures revealed that the upper classes and the growing middle class were far outnumbered by the labouring population, and this gave added weight to their concern and above all, the question of how to treat the poor. It was almost inevitable that Disraeli's 'two nations' theory of rich and poor should develop, and eventually create class consciousness.

The poor as such were not only large in number, but also diverse within such a grouping. Between the skilled craftsman, the unskilled labourer, and also between the young, the elderly, the single man and the married man with a large family, there were tremendous differences. Earnings were the significant factor which separated the artisan in a steady job from the labourer, subject to the threat of unemployment. The elderly, with reduced or no earning power, had little to fall back on: and the young married man, once his children were born, no longer had his wife's earnings to supplement the family income. For a great many of the labouring class, the only time in their lives when they had earnings to spare was before marriage and in middle age once the children had begun to earn a wage for themselves.

The highly skilled artisans, the cabinet makers, jewellers, printers, watchmakers, shipwrights, locomotive engineers and fine spinners and dyers – men who had served a lengthy apprenticeship in their own craft – regarded themselves as equal with the lower middle classes, the clerks and shop assistants.

Factory workers were a substantial group among the unskilled workforce, but as we have seen, in 1851 agriculture absorbed over a million in labouring jobs and a further 360,000 as indoor farm servants. Much has been written of the plight of the factory operative, and justifiably so, but the sheer drudgery of most jobs on the land has been overlooked. Irish immigrants who flooded into England after the failure of the potato crop in 1845 also joined the ranks of the unskilled, and had to accept whatever job they could get: invariably low paid for long hours, and physically demanding, either on the land, or as railway navvies or dock labourers. In cities and large towns, the unskilled were employed as dustmen, scavengers and lamplighters, while 130,000 accepted the Queen's shilling and joined the army, serving either at home or abroad. In the coalfields, nearly 120,000 worked as miners where work was not only back-breakingly hard, but dangerous, and these mining communities, usually in semi-rural areas, tended to be self-contained but heavily dependent upon a single industry. For the large majority of unskilled workers, unemployment was an ever-present threat, over which they had no control. Periods of bad weather meant many thousands of those employed in agriculture and building were laid off. Industrial injuries and old age took their toll, and forced them to seek poor relief.

It could be argued that the coming of industrialisation provided more opportunities for employment and thus an improvement in the standard of living of the working classes. But this is too simplistic, for the growth in population, the casual nature of much employment and the periodic booms and slumps in the economy up to the 1850s, meant that most workers found no improvement in their general living standard.

Most of what we know of their daily lives comes from the many reports of Government select committees, royal commissions and philanthropic societies which were produced by the well-intentioned during the 1830s and 1840s. How they really felt is not so clear, for as a class they were largely inarticulate and above all bewildered at the speed of change.

Again, personal circumstances differed widely between the skilled and the unskilled. In towns, most people lived in two-storey houses, usually in terraces or around a central courtyard. These were rented and varied from two rooms and a cellar, back to back, sharing a privy, to the 'two-up two-down' which opened straight on to the street. But there were also those who could afford only a cellar dwelling or a room in a local lodging house. In the more salubrious parts of the towns lived the skilled workers whose houses were less cramped, often with a yard or small garden at the back; and some of these dwellings can still be found to this day in many industrial towns. None of these houses had any indoor sanitation, streets were unpaved and ill-lit, and there was no adequate water supply for working class housing was invariably provided in low-lying parts of the towns where drainage was poor, and sewerage and the provision of piped water was difficult, and therefore costly to install. Inevitably, such living conditions were breeding grounds for infectious diseases such as typhoid, cholera and smallpox.

Living conditions in rural areas were little better. Cottages were usually two rooms at ground level and two above, mainly brick-built, but older houses of wattle and daub still existed, and few provided more than the basic needs: the only redeeming feature being the absence of the smoke which hung over the industrial towns.

Family diet for most people was stodgy and monotonous, with a heavy reliance on bread, potatoes and weak tea, with meat or bacon two or three times a week. In bad times, many suffered from semi-starvation. In any case, the wives of labourers had often only an open fire or a simple oven for cooking, and if they too were working, little time to prepare elaborate meals. It was not until the second half of the century that the average diet improved.

The factory system had a profound effect on the family life of the working class. No longer were members of the family together at home, working on the land and often combining this with handloom weaving. Going to work in the mill meant that the family was only together to sleep, eat and on Sundays and holidays. If the wife went out to work, she had little time to cook, clean and care for the children, and young unmarried girls had little opportunity to learn any domestic skills. It was also alleged that life in the mills induced sexual immorality and licentiousness. The father's role too was diminished when he was not the only breadwinner in the family, and on occasions might be out of work, when his wife and children had jobs in the mill.

Whereas the working classes benefited little from the national wealth which industrialisation brought, for the middle classes and the landowners the picture was very different. The ownership of land provided stability and a traditional way of life and authority, and for the ambitious upper middle class it indicated success. Yet both the aristocracy and the gentry had to adapt to their changing role. The peerage retained its authority and leadership, either by intermarrying within its own closely-knit social group of titled families, or seeking alliances with bankers and industrialists. Judicious investment in railways, coal-mining and property in the industrial centres brought additional wealth. The gentry too maintained its social prestige at local and county level, through the magistrates' bench and its obligations to its tenant farmers and neighbours. Through primogeniture they kept their estates intact and individual, while their younger sons took up careers in business and the professions. Profitable marriages helped too and enabled the ambitious entrepreneur to join their ranks for the social prestige which it afforded.[12]

The middle classes, with their new-found wealth, were above all else eager to become part of this 'genteel' way of life, but as with the labouring classes, there were wide differences within their ranks. As we have seen, the wealthiest became accepted by the upper classes. The rest, to some extent, conscious of their association with 'trade', were particularly aware of their class and as a result set themselves standards of hard work and morality which we still today regard as 'Victorian values'. A steady income, a house of suitable size and in the right area, furnished accordingly and with a servant or two, enabled them to eat and to dress as advocated in the countless books on domestic economy which became essential reading for every middle-class wife. Thus the middle-class family came to be seen as exerting a moral restraining influence upon its members which was a highly desirable model for the lower classes to emulate. For women, marriage was regarded as the only goal in life. Yet, expected to be totally subservient to her husband, and with the housework performed by servants, the middle class woman invariably led a trivial and boring existence. For single women, the future was bleak, either looking after elderly parents, living in a married brother or sister's home, or taking work as a governess, which was little more than a genteel form of domestic service – Jane Eyre had found this to her cost when Mr Rochester's house-guests saw her in the sitting room shadows. But the social and moral disciplines which the Victorian middle-class family exerted on its members was in reality far from ideal. It was a male-dominated world in which women had no acceptable part to play outside marriage. The part played by religious observance further enhanced the Victorians' moralistic attitude to all aspects of family and social life.

Given time, the material effects of industrialisation, urban over-crowding, poor housing, inadequate sanitation and the rest, could be remedied. What took much longer to come to terms with were the intangible effects of the complete change in society from a rural to an urban-based community. The impetus for change lay with the growing middle class who played a dominant role in urban life. Conscious of their success in spearheading the coming of an industrial society, they inevitably sought to inculcate in others those values which they regarded as having made themselves successful. This was epitomised by Samuel Smiles in his book *Self Help*, published in 1859, which stemmed from a series of lectures he gave in the 1840s to a 'self-improvement' group in Leeds. He emphasized the virtues of thrift, punctuality, personal orderliness and the use of leisure for constructive purposes. Smiles' book was full of worthy homilies – 'Satan finds mischief for idle hands', 'Take care of the pennies and the pounds will take care of themselves' and 'Where there's a will there's a way'. In effect for the working classes, bereft of the old social order, the way to success in the new was by self-improvement to eventual respectability. Conversely, however, this implied that lack of success in life was due to laziness and lack of moral restraint. Self-help appealed to some sections of the working class, in particular the skilled artisans and especially those who were literate.

Ironically, it was this group which had produced the working-class leaders who were to press for political and social reform between 1830 and 1850.

The pressure for reform came in many guises and not only from the working class, which at this stage was inarticulate and lacking in identity.

The need for the reform of the electoral basis of parliamentary representation had been simmering for many years before the Reform Bill of 1832. The extension of the franchise to middle-class householders in the towns and to smaller tenant farmers in the countryside was less significant than the redistribution of parliamentary seats to encompass the big new industrial towns. The Act however went only so far, and left many dissatisfied and eager for further reforms.

The rise of the Chartist movement was an attempt to improve social conditions by means of political reform. The Chartists' aims were sound enough for they felt that a House of Commons comprised of landowners, capitalists and manufacturers could never understand or accede to the demands of the working classes: therefore further reform of the House was essential if their needs were to be met. Their six-point charter, issued in 1838, required universal male suffrage, annual parliaments, secret ballots, the abolition of the property qualification for MPs, the payment of MPs and equal electoral districts. Yet it was not a national movement; rather it reflected particular grievances at local level. It attracted skilled artisans who had been striving to establish trade unions to defend and consolidate the skills of colleagues.

An ambitious venture, headed by Robert Owen, the industrialist who had set up his model factory at New Lanark, established the Grand National Consolidated Trades Union. Its utopian aims were dashed by the verdict of transportation on the six Tolpuddle Martyrs who, in 1834, were convicted of administering illegal oaths at their trade union meeting. Chartism also allied with the distressed handloom weavers of Lancashire who saw the movement as an anti-capitalist organisation. The Chartists encompassed many shades of radical and social opinion, from the socialist utopianism of the Owenites to the militancy of the mill operatives. Never before had mass rallies and processions on such a scale been held. For those in government the fear of revolution was very real. Chartism failed to achieve its aims, but it brought together and united all shades of radical opinion, and from this distillation there grew a strength, conviction and class consciousness among those who up to this time had been regarded merely as the 'labouring poor'. By 1851, however, the passion which Chartism had engendered had ebbed away. In that year, the Great Exhibition celebrated the success of Britain's industrial supremacy and the thousands who went to the Crystal Palace gaped and wondered at it all. The economy was in a more stable condition and most workers had come to accept the discipline of the factory and had found a basic security and fellowship which the friendly societies now provided.

If Chartism produced in the working man a sense of class-consciousness, the Anti-Corn Law League, which began in 1838, provided the middle class with a focal pont to attack the pre-eminence of the landowners. The League, headed by a group of Manchester radicals, wanted to abolish the Corn Laws, which taxed imported grain, and consequently in poor harvest years put up the price of food, while protecting the landowning interest. 'Free Trade' became their slogan and through a nation-wide campaign they gradually won support. The potato famine in Ireland in 1845 gave them the opportunity they needed to get a bill to repeal the Corn Laws passed by Parliament in the following year.

This effectively ended the economic policy which up to 1846 had consisted of the imposition of a whole series of restrictive import duties which were totally at variance with the views of men like Cobden and Bright in Manchester, who preached *laissez faire* and complete freedom of trade and competitive enterprise. Free Trade particularly appealed therefore to the new breed of factory owners and industrialists and became the watch word for Victorian middle-class liberalism. But there was a price to pay. Customs and excise duties on imports had provided much of our revenue. Now income tax was to take their place.

Looking back on the years from 1800 to 1850, Britain's world position had grown immeasurably. She had remained at peace in Europe and had become the first industrial nation. Her democratic institutions had weathered the storm, tempered by the Great Reform Bill, whereas the rest of Europe had been torn by revolutions in 1830 and 1848. Chartism had focussed attention on the social effects of industrialism, which writers and radical thinkers further exposed, bringing about a new social awareness at home and abroad. In 1833 slavery was abolished in the British colonies, and gradually with a more liberal colonial policy Canada, Australia and New Zealand acquired responsible self-government. So much had been achieved in just fifty years. Yet so much had still be done. Jeremy Bentham (1748–1832), had propounded his philosophy that legislation should provide 'the greatest happiness to the greatest number' and among his followers *laissez faire* had been regarded as the way to achieve this end. By 1850 however, the negative approach of *laissez faire* had to yield to a more interventionist policy. Social conditions created by industrialisation which had induced the Hammonds to write,[13] in 1917:

Hence it was that amid all the conquests over nature that gave its triumph to the Industrial Revolution, the soul of man was passing into a colder exile ... this had to be addressed. As we shall see later, there was still much to be achieved – 'By 1851, English society was only half-way to its modern pattern ... The traditional mould, if not yet completely shattered, had been severely chipped and cracked ... there could be no going back ...[14]

CHAPTER THREE

"Custom was killed and habit shaken"

LANCASHIRE was the birthplace of the first industrial revolution. Its 'dark satanic mills' have inspired countless writers and political theorists, portraying its inventors, its thrusting entrepreneurs and the misery of its workers and their horrendous living conditions. But this is not the whole story. 'Cotton Lancashire' centred on Manchester, and Liverpool with its dominance in trade and as the fulcrum of the chemical, coal-mining and salt-refining industries in its hinterland, spread their influences widely over south and south-east Lancashire. But north of the Ribble and in Furness, Lancashire remained agricultural and untouched by the coming of industrialisation, and largely remains so today.

Cotton was the catalyst which hastened industrialisation. The mechanisation of the spinning process by the introduction of the jenny, the water-frame and the mule, and the harnessing of steam created the economies of large-scale production. By the 1790s Liverpool had begun to dominate the import/export trade in raw cotton and finished cloth. The early textile entrepreneurs, already experienced in the domestic 'putting-out' system, found that buildings and machinery could be rented or hired relatively cheaply.

The Old Mill, Longton. The Mill and its adjacent house were situated on Liverpool Road. They were demolished and new houses were erected on the site in 2001–02.

With the introduction of the power-loom, the transition to a totally factory-based industry was complete.

The improvement in transportation, with the expansion of the canal network, and later the coming of the railways, financed by local landowners and also by coal-owners and industrialists, provided the essential access to raw materials and distribution of finished products. Meanwhile investment, largely by Liverpool businessmen, led to the development of coal-mining in the Wigan and St Helens areas, later followed by copper-smelting, glass-making and chemical processing.[15] One industry fed upon another, responding to increasing demand and fostered by the attraction of outside capital.

As we saw in the last chapter, between 1801 and 1851 the country's population had almost doubled. Lancashire's population had by 1851 trebled to two million, noticeably in the Manchester cotton area, where the population quadrupled, on a scale never before seen outside London. In 1861, 384,000 (211,000 being women) were employed in Lancashire's cotton mills and a further 426,000 in ancillary jobs such as mechanics and warehouse work.[16]

The power base of the old landed aristocracy and the professional middle class was threatened by the new competitive entrepreneurial middle class. But rich pickings could be made by landowners through mining concessions and ground rents in the cotton towns, and for younger sons acceptable connections were made through business or marriage with the local well-established merchant and trading families. But great landowners such as the Earl of Derby, who had previously dominated parliamentary representation in Lancashire, gradually gave way to those in commerce and industry. At local level, more and more magistrates were recruited from the mill-owning class, and in towns such as Preston, those who had made their money in industry and trade came to dominate the borough hierarchies. Thomas Miller of Horrockses Miller, cotton manufacturers, became a Preston alderman, and Thomas Leach, hosier and draper, town councillor and active in the life of Preston, were examples of this new middle class. Evidence of this can still be seen in the houses which they built in and around Winckley Square, which even today has an aura of the elegance which their Victorian wealth and prestige achieved.

The wealth created by the coming of industrialisation did not by and large benefit the working classes, who, although essential to the new economy, bore the brunt of the social change which ensued. The complete unpredictability of the new labour market left them bewildered and resentful.

Up to 1833 child labour was used extensively and was supplemented by Poor Law apprentices from London and the home counties. Penwortham Mill which had opened in the 1780s on a site in Factory Lane, now Vernon Carus Ltd, employed, in its early days, children from the London Foundling Hospital.[17]

Although they attended Walton-le-Dale church each Sunday, clad in their brown coats with yellow collars and cuffs, they worked in conditions to which 'nothing but West Indian slavery can bear analogy'.[18] For many in the cotton areas, their children's wages were a significant contribution to the family's living standards. After 1833, children under eight were forbidden to work in factories, and those between eight and thirteen were limited to working six hours a day as 'part-timers', and as a result, work for women increased. 40% of all girls in Lancashire between the ages of fifteen and nineteen were employed in cotton mills in 1851. For married women, work in the cotton trade was a cyclical experience which they abandoned once they had dependent children and returned to again when the children were older. Women's wages were a vital part of the family income when the husband's wage was irregular or insufficient, as frequently happened. Contemporary evidence stressed the evils of child-minding and the use of opiates to keep children quiet while their mothers worked in the factory. But Anderson[19] found that family and neighbourhood relationships were maintained, and that the family was able to adapt more easily to town life when relatives and previous neighbours, having already made the move, were available to help find work and lodgings and look after small children. Indeed in 1851, 70% of Preston's adult population was born outside the town, and 40% of these had come from less than ten miles away. Whatever the circumstances however, the Lancashire working class family had to change.

It is almost impossible to generalise about the improvement or otherwise of the living standards of the Lancashire working class family up to the mid-1850s. Wage differentials in the cotton industry, especially between spinners and weavers, and between those families where wife and children supplemented the income and those where they did not: and between house rents and food prices which fluctuated widely across the county account for considerable variations. But what is undisputed is the effect which the trade cycle had on almost every family, resulting in a constant fear of unemployment.

Urban housing in the cotton towns was horrendous by present-day standards, and showed little improvement until the 1840s. In the early days, over-crowding was the major problem in town centre properties, formerly inhabited by middle class residents, which were sub-divided and where sewerage and water supply were consequently totally inadequate. In this respect, Liverpool was by far the worst example, where rents were higher than elsewhere, exacerbated by the immigration of the Irish during the mid-1840s. Gradually the new municipal authorities began to get to grips with the situation, even though much of the new housing was unplanned and built by small speculative building firms. In the county's rural areas, housing conditions were better. The use of stone and slate for building provided substantial long-term dwellings, although in the Fylde and Leyland areas, mud and thatch – 'clat and clay' – still persisted until the use of bricks became more widespread by mid-century. Before the, heavy taxes on bricks made it easy for builders to erect poor-quality dwellings.[20]

The rural labourer could often eke out his wages with produce from his rented cottage garden. Although young married people and teenagers tended to move to the towns, their parents, lacking the keen-eyed sight and steady hands for work in the mills, remained in the villages in which they had been born and grew up. In any case, wage differentials between town and country were less marked. The intense demand for labour in urban areas made it necessary to pay adequate agricultural wages in the surrounding rural districts to prevent a drift from the land. A Select Committee on Labourers' Wages in 1824 found that in the Leyland area wages varied between 9s. and 15s. a week and were comparable with those paid to textile workers. Nevertheless the rural labourer was very dependent upon the weather conditions, and between 1821 and 1822 agriculture was severely depressed in the Preston area.

The workforce in the towns lived, during periods of full employment, on a diet of bread, potatoes and occasionally meat. The imposition of short-time working however, had an immediate effect on the family's nutritional standards. The agricultural labourer also relied heavily on potatoes as a staple diet, but in good times could supplement this with meat and milk.

In towns where workers lived close together and were usually employed at the same factory, a mutual relationship grew up whereby one would help another, especially when times were bad.[21] Friendly societies, pubs and burial clubs provided insurance against sickness and disability, with conviviality and a decent funeral at the end of it all.[22] Public houses and beer houses proliferated, especially after the Beerhouses Act of 1830, and regular drinking was a way of life for a large majority of the working class, despite the efforts of the temperance movement led by Joseph Livesey of Preston in 1835. The working class worked hard and played hard, not only drinking, but cock-fighting, pigeon flying and boisterous activity during the annual wakes weeks: prostitution was regarded as the 'Great Social Evil'.[23] 'Respectable' public opinion was increasingly concerned by the growing level of violence and unrest in society. The Peterloo Massacre of 1819, when a crowd of some 60,000 well-intentioned people assembled in St Peter's Fields, Manchester to hear Henry Hunt, the radical speaker, was dispersed by the local mounted yeomanry, indicated the level of nervous tension among local magistrates. Eleven were killed and 400, including many women, were injured. Further instances of tension led to the Luddite machine wrecking of 1826 and 1829 and to the Plug Plot of 1842, when wage reductions caused by depressed market conditions led striking workers to pull the plugs on mill engine boilers. The unrest began in Ashton and Stalybridge, spread to Manchester and eventually engulfed the whole of the cotton area, including Chorley and Preston. In most areas, the police and military acted with restraint, but in Lune Street, Preston, soldiers and strikers clashed causing seven of the strikers to be wounded, two of whom later died from their injuries. This did little to ease the situation which at the time many regarded as a class war. Indeed, Disraeli, writing his novel *Sybil* in 1845, considered that England consisted of 'Two Nations', the rich and the poor. Society, certainly up to 1850, was violent and crime, at least in the towns, had risen alarmingly.

The administration of justice was carried out through Justices of the Peace at the Quarter Sessions held at Preston, Salford, Lancaster and Kirkdale four times each year. By 1838, the large boroughs of Bolton, Manchester, Liverpool and Wigan had established their own Quarter Session courts. Before the establishment of a county police force, the maintenance of law and order had been carried out largely through a system which had its origins in medieval times. High constables in the hundreds (Longton lay in the Leyland hundred) and petty constables in the parishes were ostensibly responsible for the rule of law. Constables were elected by the local court leet, but the huge population increase, its concentration in the new urban areas and the rapid rise in crime made their job a thankless task.[24] Many did not want the job, and often paid somebody else to do it for them. The militia, controlled by the Lord Lieutenant, frequently had to be used to restore law and order as at Peterloo. Some Lancashire boroughs formed their own police forces as Preston did in 1815 and Lancaster in 1824. The establishment of the Metropolitan Police Force by Sir Robert Peel in 1829, and the Municipal Corporations Act of 1835, obliged other boroughs, such as Wigan and Bolton, to do the same. However, this did not deal with the increase in crime outside the borough areas, and we shall look at this in more detail when considering Longton in 1851.

Inexorably, central and local government, despite the Victorian attitude of *laissez faire*, was being drawn in to regulating the lives of the ordinary man. Two issues, the provision for the poor, and the improved public health, demanded attention, and radicals both inside and outside Parliament wanted urgent action.

The Poor Laws, since their inception in Elizabethan times, and especially the act of 1601, made each parish responsible for its poor. The overseers of the poor levied a rate which was used for the relief of the elderly, the sick and the unemployed, and for centuries it had been acknowledged that those afflicted by poverty needed more than the occasional charitable hand-outs. But by 1800 the number of those eligible for relief had grown alarmingly, and for the next thirty years the question of how to reduce the rate burden, which fell primarily on farmers in rural areas and the middle class in the towns, was discussed without any satisfactory solution. Many townships had built their own local workhouses, largely occupied by the aged and infirm, unmarried mothers and their children and orphans. Where possible, because it was cheaper to administer, the able-bodied poor were provided with outdoor relief, either through cottage rents, fuel and food, or cash payments.

By the early 1830s, a Royal Commission was set up to look into the whole question of poverty, and its report was to become the basis for the Poor Law Amendment Act of 1834.[25]

The new law, while accepting that the poor were entitled to assistance, laid down stricter conditions for the granting of relief. The 'out-door' relief was abolished and claimants were in new-style workhouses. The old parish workhouses were discontinued and replaced by a central workhouse to serve a 'union' or group of parishes. All applicants were subjected to a workhouse test, and once there, conditions were grim, the intention being to deter all but the most 'deserving' from receiving help. Those admitted were segregated into male, female and children's sections, and all were issued with the drab workhouse uniform. Conditions were comfortless and food was plain and monotonous. The able-bodied were employed in stone-breaking or picking oakum, i.e. unravelling old rope to use in caulking the decks of ships. The new law was

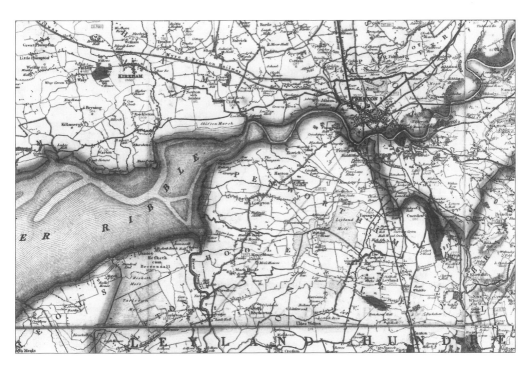

Greenwood's Map of 1818 shows the mainly agricultural area south of Preston before the onslaught of the Industrial Revolution.

largely intended to deal with the farming areas of the south east of England, where poverty was endemic, and was seen as irrelevant to Lancashire's needs.[26]

Resistance came not only from the working classes, but from local worthies who resented being dictated to by the Poor Law Commissioners, the local agents of central government, and thought that the old system was more adequate and certainly cheaper. As a result Lancashire was slow to adopt the new system which did not address the real problem of the worker on short-time who needed temporary help until conditions improved. Sadly the act dealt with results of poverty and in no way attempted to eradicate its causes. Certainly a middle-class Parliament, imbued with the Victorian notion that poverty was caused by wickedness and lack of drive, had no understanding of, in particular, the independent spirit of the Lancashire operative. Consequently the law came to be regarded as legislation made by the 'haves' to regulate the 'have-nots', and the bitterness it created lasted the best part of a hundred years.

The inadequacies of public health were revealed by Edwin Chadwick's *Report on the Sanitary condition of the Labouring Population of Great Britain* and which culminated in the Public Health Act of 1848.[27]

Liverpool had the worst conditions of any town in Lancashire, but Preston also exhibited the chronic living state of the typical Lancashire cotton town, and was regarded by Engels as one of the most squalid places he had visited. In 1846 53% of its children under the age of five died, and in 1849, 5,000 inhabitants died during the cholera epidemic of that year. Indeed, when Charles Dickens wrote *Hard Times* he based his fictitious 'Coketown' on Preston with its terraces of houses separated by backyards which contained the privy, cess-pit or ashpit, irregularly cleaned out by 'scavengers'. Most houses had no running water, and sewers were not constructed until the 1850s. Diseases such as cholera and typhus were endemic. Gradually local authorities such as Preston established their own Boards of Health which laid down stricter building regulations, and tackled the problems of slum clearance, the removal of nuisances, street widening and gas lighting. Yet, because the law was permissive rather than mandatory, the speed with which improvements were made varied considerably from one authority to another. Liverpool and Manchester, admittedly with the worst conditions, dealt with them with determination: Bury, largely because of its local property-owners' opposition, had a less commendable record at least until 1870.

By mid-century, the property-owning class benefited from the general expansion of trade and it became relatively easy to accumulate wealth, despite the temporary financial crisis of 1848, mainly caused by over-exuberant speculation in railway shares. The working classes however saw no real improvement in their daily lives until the 1870s.

Lancashire's cotton industry, always prey to endemic booms and slumps, suffered particularly in 1853/54 and again in 1861/65. Before 1853 there had been a rapid trade expansion and new mills were built in the cotton areas. Preston by 1852 had sixty-four mills in operation, expanding its markets for shirtings and fancy goods to India and China. Preston weavers felt that they too should benefit from the increased prosperity, and when offered a wage increase of 5% they refused it and adopted their motto 'Ten Percent and No Surrender'.[28] In retrospect it was a bitter affair with neither side victorious. The weavers, led by George Cowell, went on strike and persisted in their claim for 10% and were supported by weavers from other towns who contributed to a strike fund for their Preston colleagues. The mill owners refused to meet the strike delegates and eventually in September 1853 announced a general 'lock-out', which apart from a dozen or so employers, affected 80% of the town's factories. The owners were completely out of sympathy with the strikers, declaring their meetings 'mischievous interference and terrorism'. They believed that wage increases were dependent upon supply and demand, and that their authority as masters was paramount. The weavers for their part sorely misjudged the timing of the strike. The cotton boom of 1848/52 had collapsed, mainly due to the loss of the China market caused by internal rebellion by the Chinese nationalists against the ruling dynasty and the closure of Shanghai to imports from Britain. The mill owners tried to bring in black-leg labour by canvassing the Manchester area, the Belfast workhouse and even agricultural labourers from Buckinghamshire, but this failed, for many of these imported labourers left or were found to be quite unsuitable for the work involved. Eventually in May 1854 the strike collapsed, in large measure due to the dwindling support from other cotton towns whose weavers were on short-time working.

Cotton operatives suffered far worse deprivations during the 'Cotton Famine' of 1861/65, due to the blockade on the export of raw cotton from the southern states during the American Civil War. By November 1861, 81,000 Lancashire workers were unemployed and 12,000 on poor relief.[29] The 'labour test', which required that relief should only be given if applicants were willing to be set to work and accepted relief in the form of tickets which could only be spent at selected shops, was bitterly resented, for many were totally unsuited to the hard manual work which was offered. Conditions worsened in 1862–63, for many, unable to pay their rents, had to move to cheaper houses or become homeless; others pawned their few possessions to buy food, and small shop-keepers went out of business. In Preston 38.8% of the town's population was receiving poor relief, and it was clear that the system could not cope with the unprecedented demands made upon it. Late in 1862, Lord Derby set up a Central Executive Committee to provide additional funds and later, through the efforts of Sir James Kaye-Shuttleworth, the Committee secretary, the rest of England began to contribute to the relief fund. Soup kitchens were set up and clothes and bedding were distributed from local centres. Operatives were induced by cash allowances to attend local 'work schools' where women were taught reading, writing and simple sewing, and the men were taught shoemaking, carpentry and reading. Meanwhile there was considerable criticism levelled at seventy-one Preston mill owners who only collected £1,800 towards the relief of the plight of their workers, In Blackburn it was even worse, and only £700 was collected from ninety-one mill owners. The Government, while welcoming voluntary effort, stuck to its *laissez faire* policy of non-intervention by insisting on the 'labour test' and encouraging public works such as drainage schemes, street-paving and laying out of public parks. Some of Preston's parks were constructed at this time. MPs were also urging the offer of cheap assisted passages to Australia to those who wished to go, but there were few takers and most Lancashire workers stuck it out, until the resumption of cotton imports in 1865. To Westminster's relief, unrest in Lancashire during the famine was minimal. Indeed Preston Corporation held its Guild in 1862 to provide at least some lighter relief for its townsfolk, even though it 'presented the strange contrast of a carnival and a famine'. Lord Shaftesbury summarised the country's recognition of Lancashire's powers of endurance: 'There is nothing finer on earth than a Lancashire man or a Lancashire woman.'

By the 1870s the standard of living for most of Lancashire's working class had improved. The cost of basic foodstuffs fell. Bread, tea and sugar prices halved between 1874 and 1894 and cheap meat was easier to obtain. The continued employment of women in the cotton industry enabled families in these areas to enjoy a greater element of choice in their spending power when trade was good, and to 'put something by for a rainy day'. However, Liverpool did not share in this improvement. The casual nature of its dock employment and the lack of opportunities for women's work, other than poorly paid jobs, left the city with a considerable under-class of families who lived below the poverty line. In the cotton areas, better housing, slum clearance, piped water and the beginnings of public health care began to provide a better environment in which to live. Confidence grew and municipal authorities all over Lancashire demonstrated their civic pride in the town halls, museums and libraries which they built. Preston's Town Hall, designed by Sir George Gilbert Scott, was built on Fishergate in 1867 and the Harris Museum and Library in 1882–83. Manchester Town Hall, designed by Alfred Waterhouse in the Gothic style, was completed in 1877 and the Free Trade Hall in 1856.[30]

Although Lancashire cotton towns had a long way to go to mitigate their smoke-laden atmosphere, their grimy buildings and pockets of poor quality housing, their inhabitants felt more secure and confident, largely due to the slow but steady improvement in their living standards. Statutory public holidays and the five-and-a-half-day week enabled the working class to look outside its immediate neighbourhood for entertainment. Public houses and theatres had wide appeal. Pubs provided not only drink, but food and 'singing saloons' which were popular with the younger generation, and there was also bowling, wrestling, skittles and cards. Theatres widened their attraction and offered not only plays, but minstrel shows and music hall entertainment which provided down-to-earth humour and sentimental songs which reflected day-to-day life and Victorian romantic aspirations.[31]

Meanwhile in rural Lancashire, life went on much as before. Landowners invested in expensive drainage schemes, but these were insufficient, despite the new urban markets, to stave off the depression which affected agriculture nationally at the end of the century, caused by imports from America, Russia, Denmark and Australia. While the small farmer continued to use mainly family labour, many left the land, never to return. In Lancashire in 1851, 36,000 were employed in agriculture, but by 1911 this had fallen to 20,000. Even so, rural wages improved, primarily to deter workers from migrating to the towns.[32] Living standards improved, but many villages saw stagnation in population until the turn of the century when improved transportation brought an influx, at least in larger villages, of tradesmen – brewers, grocers, blacksmiths, carriers and some professional people. Nevertheless self-sufficiency, which had been so much a part of village life, gradually came to an end. Religion was no longer the focus it had been. The farm labourer had distanced himself from the dependence on his landlord and women saw a visit to the nearby town as a welcome break from village frustrations. But the village child still had a very different upbringing from his or her urban counterpart.[33] Children had room to play outdoors and could roam the countryside freely, climb the trees or go fishing, at least in their early years. As we shall see later, the Education Acts passed between

1870 and 1880 enforced the attendance at school of every child over five, but the law was imperfectly applied and for various reasons, children were still employed extensively in farm work, particularly on a seasonal basis.

By the end of the century, Lancashire had undergone a profound and irreversible change. In the south-eastern and central areas, and in Liverpool, the landscape and its society had witnessed momentous upheaval, but in the rural areas its influence was limited. For many, vast fortunes had been made, but for others speculation had resulted in penury. Those caught up by industrialisation exchanged the old rural interdependent deferential society for a new urban regime which was equally deferential and dependent. *Laissez-faire* remained paramount and the guiding rule of Victorian social philosophy at least until the 1880s, when doubt and criticism began to corrode its belief in 'progress' and improvement. By 1900 the reforms which the Victorians had hailed as innovative and far-reaching had become out-worn and demanded total reconstruction.

ERNESS HUNDR

Sowerby

Bilsborough

Inglenhite

Longley

Barton

Barton Hall

Black Hall

Mills

Eaves

Lawrence Chapel

Goosnargh

Inskip

Mudge

Hollowforth

Whit

Middleton

Rigby Esq

Gingle Hall

Haighton

Roseacre

Wharles

Catforth

Black Pole

Bell Fold

Crow Hall

Newsham Hall

Four Lane

Shuttleworth Esq

Barton Lodge

Whittingham Hall

Fedder Esq

Treales

Wood Plumpton

Crown Lane

Hough

Broughton

Durton

Haighton

Mowbrick Hall

Bartell

Higher Tower

Laighforth Houses

Broughton Tower

Haighton House

Salwick

Roundabout Smithy

Moor Hall

Rawsterne Esq

Black Bull

Fulwood

Ingoll

Cottam

Leach Hall

Cottam Hall

Fulwood Hall

Clifton

Newton

Scales

Lea

Alston

PRESTON

Ribble

Freckleton

Lea Hall House

Howick

Penwortham

Walton

Wall

Hutton

School

Hutton Hall

Longton

White Stakes

Lostock Hall

Hall Green

Walmer Bridge

Little Hoole

Moss

Farington

Cuerden

Clayton

Hesketh Bank

Becconsall

Much Hoole

Bretherton

Leyland

Clayton Hall

Tarleton

Croston

Eccleston

EYLAND HUN

Ulnes Walton

Euxton

CHAPTER FOUR

A Working Village

⁊HE FIRST Ordnance Survey maps provides us with a snapshot
of the village as it was between 1844 and 1845.

William Yates had surveyed the village in 1786, following John
Speed's map of 1610 and Saxton's of 1577. George Hennett also
produced his map between 1828 and 1829, but valuable as these
early maps are in showing the gradual linear development of the
village, none have the accuracy and detail which the Victorian
Ordnance Survey cartographers produced.

Longton today is largely a creation of the second half of the
twentieth century. Before then, the village was a settlement which
had developed gradually over the centuries from earliest times.

The landscape was formed around 10,000 years ago, by boulder
clay washed down from the Lake District and the Pennines in
the last Ice Age. Earliest vegetation was buried to form extensive
peat bogs which lie to the east and south of the village and which,
following reclamation from swamp and marsh in the eighteenth
century, provided some of the most fertile soils in England.

The village was, and still is, a straggling settlement on either
side of the three main roads – Liverpool Road, Marsh Lane and
Chapel Lane. Indeed its Anglo-Saxon name *Longetuna* means a

Opposite: Yates' Map of 1786.

long village, and accurately describes its straggling form. The three roads significantly all lie on a ridge of boulder clay, giving a drained causeway above the level of the fields and mosses on either side.

So geological factors governed Longton's development, influencing the housing density along its main thoroughfares and inhibiting its spread eastwards and southwards until drainage had been achieved. Housing spread gradually in a linear fashion, with in-filling of the remaining plots as the years went by.

Longton had always been an 'open village', that is to say a community where there was no resident lord of the manor, who would have controlled where his tenants could live. Instead, housing grew in response to need. The parish is extensive – some 3,383 acres, and larger than any of its neighbours. Penwortham has 2,270 acres, Hutton 2,576, and the Hooles, 2,993 acres.

In the medieval period therefore, land was not in short supply, and people built their cottages each with their individual plots or crofts extending at the rear. Behind these ran Back Lane which separated the crofts from the open field strips which extended to the parish boundary of Longton Brook. These are very clearly shown on the Ordnance Survey maps.

This medieval layout, centuries old by 1851, remained largely unchanged until the major housing developments of the 1960s. Then Longton doubled in size, was by-passed by a new section of the A59 and developed into a community village serving Preston and Leyland.

But the core of the village has remained. Liverpool Road, the main thoroughfare between Preston and Liverpool, had existed even before the turnpike road was established in 1771. Marsh Lane, as its name implies, led down to the marsh itself, giving access not only to cottages along its length, but to the marsh where we

Opposite: Hennett's Map of 1828–29.

know that in 1797, goods were off-loaded from vessels in the rivers Ribble and Asland. It may have been significant from even earlier times, for local people still talk of a Roman road at Bartle Brow, and a road which ran between Walton-le-Dale, where there was a Roman settlement, and Longton Marsh. It is not inconceivable that the marsh at Longton could have provided access to the Roman fort at Kirkham, directly across the river Ribble. In the same way, Chapel Lane, leading eastwards, connected the old village settlement with the farms which grew up after the drainage of Longton Moss in the eighteenth century, but it too may have been an ancient route connecting Longton with the Roman settlement at Walton-le-Dale. At first sight, it appears that Chapel Lane got its name from the Primitive Methodist chapel built there in 1837. But as it appears on Saxton's map of 1577 leading to 'Longton Chapel', on the site of the present parish church, this is probably the true origin of its name.

But to return to 1851 and Longton as it was then. Many English villages have remained as if time had stood still, their original houses, church, school and perhaps a village green, all as they were two or three hundred years ago.

Longton is not like that. Some older buildings remain, but many more have gone or been extensively rebuilt and modernised. None of the early houses or farm buildings now remain. But we can get some impression of what they were like from the photograph of the cottage, known locally as the Round House. It stood on Sod Hall Lane, New Longton, until it was destroyed in a thunderstorm in 1983. The roof and walls were supported by a 'cruck' made from the split trunk of an oak tree. Timber uprights formed a frame for the walls which were thickly daubed with wet clay reinforced with straw giving a weather-proof covering. Wattle and daub was used to make the internal walls and thatch for the roof.

Gradually as the production of bricks for domestic use developed, local houses were rebuilt. Timber-framed walls were replaced by solid brick walls, extra rooms were often added, and walls were heightened to allow more headroom and use the loft space. Blackett's Farm, Brownhill Lane, which has long since gone, illustrates this rebuilding in brick, although the thatched roof remains, and some exterior walls were rendered for extra protection. Building continued throughout the eighteenth century and several houses are examples from this period. With the Victorian era, domestic

The Round House, near Hutton and Howick.

building styles changed, and Chestnut House on Liverpool Road, which dates from this period, is a good local example.

Whether a village grows or declines is clearly measured by its rise or fall in population. It is also reflected in its domestic buildings, for people had to live somewhere. But an increase in population does not necessarily mean an increase in the number of dwellings. Limitations on building and lack of money often meant that people were more closely crowded together. Neither did a fall in population necessarily result in vacant properties. Often houses were pulled down, became dilapidated or were rebuilt or extended. But given these provisos, basic conclusions can be drawn from the correlation between housing and population. The ratio between the size of population and the number of occupied houses provides the average size of household in a village at any one time. Unlike the figures for family size, household size includes servants, lodgers and even other families living in the same dwelling. In the first census of 1801, Longton's housing density was 4.9 per household. By 1841 it had risen to 5.5, but by 1851 had dropped slightly to 5.4. In 1881 it had fallen again to 4.9. Averages can be distorted by, for example, a large household where many servants are employed, or where several families lived together in over-crowded towns like Preston in the early years of the century. But in Longton these extremes did not apply and therefore the figures are more meaningful.

Using the Ordnance Survey map of 1844–45, together with the census material for 1851, it is possible even today to recreate what the village must have been like when the enumerator came to carry out the census in 1851.

Let us begin on Liverpool Road in the centre of the village.

In 1851, the road was busy, being the turnpike between Preston and Liverpool (the by-pass was only built in 1957). Farm carts of all descriptions, coaches, people on horse-back and others on foot used it. It had no macadamed surface until 1911, and so in 1851, in common with thousands of similar roads up and down the country, it was composed of compacted earth, the ruts and potholes filled in here and there with rubble and stones, with grass verges on either side. It was a quagmire in winter and a dust-bowl in summer time.

On the corner where today's Spar store now stands was Cicely Jump's grocery shop and close by was her brother Ralph's wheelwright's business. Between these lived Thomas Pickering, the Relieving Officer, who made payments in cash or kind to the paupers of the parish. Where Church Row Chambers now stands was a row of cottages called Parker's Row inhabited by several weavers and a labourer. Unfortunately the OS map is incorrect here showing Parker's Row too far to the east, next to the Ram's Head, which of course is on the south side of Liverpool Road. However in the later 1894 OS map this is corrected.

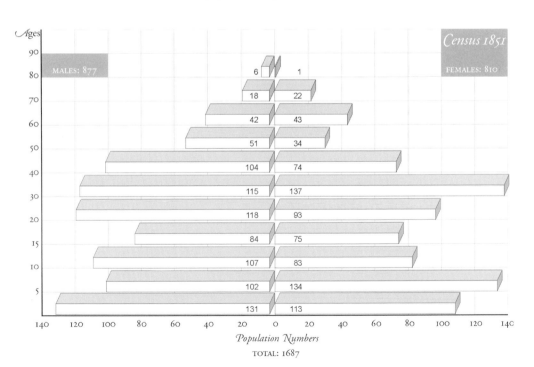

Population Numbers

TOTAL: 1687

On the east side of what is now Franklands was Parker's Farm, hence the probable connection with Parker's Row. Between Franklands and today's Booth's supermarket was the Police Station and three small cottages occupied by two weavers and a labourer. Where the present telephone exchange now stands was a house and garden. In it lived Miss Isabella Baxendale, a teacher, and her widowed sister. Lodging with them was the Rev. Jonah Nicholson, a bachelor, and the curate of Longton Chapel. Between 1810 and 1851 a succession of curates had officiated at the Chapel, and it is understood that they had previously lived in the house which is further along Liverpool Road, now called the Old Parsonage. Writing in 1872, Hewitson says 'There is no parsonage-house at Longton' and refers to the Rev. Charles Astbury, the then incumbent, living in 'a portion of the Mansion House, in the region of which must by this time have got duly consecrated for in it there lived two or three incumbents, and near it a similar number'.[34] Next to Miss Baxendale's was a fairly large house, where the Mansion House stood. It had an orchard, a garden at the front with a barn to the side, and was occupied by Robert Harrison and his family who farmed sixty acres, and was known as 'Loxam's' in 1851.

There were two cottages with gardens attached at the corner of Shirley Lane occupied by a wheelwright and a labourer, but these were later demolished when Glebe House was built in the 1900s. Where Chestnut House now stands was an earlier house, with a barn and garden surrounding it, where a farmer called Edward Taylor lived. A small cottage at the rear was unoccupied in 1851. It is believed that in 1854 the farmhouse was rebuilt and heightened in the process, but that some of the foundations of the original house were retained. The original adjacent barn was sympathetically restored in the 1970s.

Henry Hale had a shoemaker's business on what is now the corner of Lanedale, and next to him at the Manor House lived Richard Moss and his family. This house has now completely

Liverpool Road, Longton.

disappeared, and I recall when I came to live in Longton in 1971, that the site was being cleared and the last of the rubble removed, to make way for the New Manor residential home. Beyond the Manor House, the picture becomes rather confused. Richard Wilkins, the maltster and brewer, may have lived at this time at the Old Parsonage, and Mr James Newton, an elderly widower and 'proprietor of houses', could have occupied Milestone Cottage, but I have not been able to verify this. Richard Mawdsley the blacksmith lived in the vicinity, possibly at what is now Elm House, although he ran his business from the smithy in the centre of the village, opposite the entrance to the present-day library. The Red Lion was tenanted by William Whittle in 1851 and next to it, Cobble Cottage was occupied by a weaver. Beyond lived several weavers and labourers whose cottages have since disappeared. Thomas Rawcliffe, a house carpenter, may have occupied what we now call Strickson's Cottage.

At the top of Marsh Lane, on the north side, was Robert Banks' grocer's shop and next to it, a malt kiln where Peter Bibby, a brewer lived and where Malt Kiln Cottages now stand. Next door lived Ann Park who farmed sixteen acres at what is still known today as Park Farm. The Wesleyan chapel had been built in 1807 and enlarged in 1833 with the addition of a Sunday school, but was later rebuilt in 1872. Further along the lane, William Ryding kept a shop and a little further down lived Mrs Sutton, a widow, who had a baker's shop. The rest of the houses in Marsh Lane were mainly occupied by small farmers or farm labourers, each with their plot of land at the side or more frequently at the rear. Those on the north side of the lane extended at the rear, and occupied part of the medieval field strips which ran between Marsh Lane and Back Lane, and are clearly visible even on today's Ordnance Survey map. Pilot Cottage, at the end of Grange Lane, was occupied by a weaver in 1851, and the present-day Dolphin Inn was a 'beer house', where William Buck and his family lived. Although he sold beer, his main job was agricultural labouring.

Returning to Marsh Lane, the south side contained a succession of small farms and weavers' cottages, until we reach Longton Free

Pilot Cottage – taken before its conversion c. 1910.

School. The building was demolished in the 1980s but on the new building which replaced it is a replica of the original circular date stone inscribed 'Founded by Mr R. M. Moss, 1803'. Next to the school lived James Pye, the brewer. He also farmed fifty-five acres, and while his eldest son Edward helped in the brewery, his younger son James worked on the farm. In 1851, Dale Avenue did not exist, but I believe that what is now No.2 was the Pye's coachhouse. On the Ordnance Survey map there is also a reference to 'Maltings' at Whalebone Farm lower down Marsh Lane, and this may have formed part of the Pyes' brewing business. Next door to James Pye was Plumpton House where, in 1851, William Wilkins the maltster and brewer lived. Unmarried, he lived with his sister, a nephew and niece and four servants, and like James Pye, he also farmed forty acres. John Moss lived at Tithebarn Farm which lay between Plumpton House and the Golden Ball. The old tithe barn is clearly shown on the Tithe Map, next to the farmhouse and prior to the Tithe Commutation Act of 1836, would be where local farmers had to bring one tenth of their yearly profit from the soil or from farm stock, which was used to defray the expenses of the parish church. The barn and farmhouse were demolished several years ago to accommodate a residential nursing home.

In the 1838 Tithe Map, the Golden Ball, with its brewhouse and yard, had been tenanted by James Pye, but by 1851, John Wilkins, presumably a younger brother of William, had taken over the tenancy. James Wilkins, who must have been another brother, tenanted the Ram's Head. As the century progressed, the Wilkins family expanded their business, concentrating on malting and brewing, and abandoning their direct involvement with the local public houses. In 1883 they built the brewery complex on Marsh Lane – demolished in 1976 to make way for The Maltings housing development – and extended their business to Preston, at Mill Bank in Church Street. By the turn of the century the Wilkinses were of considerable consequence in the village, as we shall see in a later chapter, but the Longton branch of the family eventually died out and the estate was sold in 1928. The Pyes did not have the same business success, and by 1911 their brewery was closed.

Back to the turnpike road (Liverpool Road) we come to the cottages next to the Golden Ball. Here lived Miss Ellen Fisher, a 'landed proprietess' who was blind and aged seventy-three, and Henry Sutton, the tailor, who had his workshop further down on the opposite side of the road, and whose family continued the tailoring business in the village for many years. The row of houses now called Grove Cottages existed in 1851, and opposite stood Grove Cottage. Here lived Arthur Dawson, a cotton spinner whose mill in Preston employed 384 workers. Grove Cottage was later demolished to make way for Grove House built for the Wilkins family. Opposite the present-day Birkdale Avenue was a cornmill with an adjacent house where Thomas Barron the mill owner lived. The buildings have now been replaced by new houses. Old Mill Cottage was formerly a farmhouse, and where Blundell's hardware store now stands was the village pinfold where stray cattle were impounded. Oddfellows Cottages, now shops, were occupied in 1851 by two weavers' families and by Samuel Wilding, a tailor, whose mother Lettice lived next door and had a small business as a tripe-maker to provide for herself and her teenage son who was disabled. Robert Riley, a master clogger, lived at Rose Cottage near the Black Bull Inn. The inn had some twenty acres of land and while John Taylor ran the inn, assisted by his wife, and daughter and helped by Ellen Watkinson who served the ale, his sons and a farm servant worked on the land. The inn also provided residential accommodation, for on the day of the census a 'Mrs Nicholson' is listed as a 'traveller staying there'.

In 1851, there was an open field next to the Black Bull, for the two shops were not built until after the turn of the century. Where 'Holme Lea', 'Alderley', The Drive and 101 to 111 Liverpool Road now stand, there was a house with a barn and garden nearby, and

The Grove, now demolished.

a cottage also surrounded by a garden. The area which we now know today between West View and the corner of School Lane would be quite unrecognisable to anyone living in the village in 1851. This is because the building of St Andrew's church, and later the Church Hall, which replaced the old church, a school and about twenty-five houses and cottages, occupied the site of today's church, hall and graveyard. The chapel, built in 1773, replaced the chantry chapel, 'a small plain brick building', which had previously been on the site from the early sixteenth century. The chapel of 1773 was a 'typical small country church' and Hewitson[35] was not impressed when he visited it in 1872: 'It is an odd-looking building – a clumsy, architecturally lumpish sort of a building.' The external walls were covered in concrete or plaster, with a slate roof of the ordinary country barn type. The squat tower housed a bell and above it 'a powerful-looking spread eagle, intended to show which way the wind blows'. The church clock which had originated 'in a stable or a mechanics shop in Preston' was somewhat temperamental, even before it was sold to the chapel. Once in position it became most unreliable and a local resident observed that 'the last time I heard it, it struck ninety and kept going on till I got tired and went away'. The small graveyard was unkempt with tombstones leaning in all directions. The school, built in 1818 next to the church, served both as a Sunday school and day school. The village stocks, in which miscreants were put to teach them the error of their ways, stood nearby on land now occupied by the parking area fronting the commercial properties at the corner of School Lane.

The OS map of 1845 shows the old chapel on an island site with turnpike road on its north side and Back School Lane to the south. Surrounding the chapel on three sides was a group of properties, principally cottages, largely occupied by handloom weavers, together with a small shop and a cottage where John Taylor the school master lived with his elderly mother, and the 'old School House' on School Lane which had served as the school before 1818. Where the Church Hall now stands was a row of nine cottages called Garstang's Row, and down School Lane, near numbers 16–24, was a group of four cottages with a garden to the rear called Garstang House. Garstang's Row housed several weavers and two agricultural labourers and their families, and Garstang House was occupied by four pauper weavers' families. The Garstang connection must relate to two members of the Garstang family who had become influential in the village at this time. Thomas Garstang had bought land which had formed part of the manorial estate of the Shireburn/Weld family. By 1838 a William Garstang had purchased grazing land, and together with William Clarkson, brother-in-law of Thomas Garstang, owned some thirty cottages in and around the village of which Garstang's Row and Garstang House were part. A document listing 'cottage rents paid by the Overseers of Longton' must have included the rents paid on behalf of some of the paupers who occupied Garstang House.[36]

Beyond the church stood the Rams Head Inn, but not the building we know today. The old inn formed part of a group, with the small smithy to one side, and on the other a joiner's shop. This may explain the fact that the Mawdsleys lived at the opposite end of the village, near the Red Lion, but carried on the bulk of their business from the main smithy in the centre of the village. A little way up Chapel Lane a tithe barn had stood, opposite the track leading to Longton Hall farm. It is shown on the Tithe Map of 1838, but on the OS map of 1845 has disappeared. Presumably after the passing of the Tithe Commutation Act, there was no further need for such a building and it was demolished.

On the perimeter of the parish, drainage and land reclamation works which had been completed in 1806 resulted in the reclamation of the hinterland, notably the fields to the west of Hall Carr Lane and on either side of the Walmer Brook, and of the mossland at New Longton. Prior to the New Sea Cop, all the low-lying land to the west and south of Longton was often in danger of flooding through the combination of spring tides and north-westerly gales. The small community of Hall Green still remained somewhat isolated, but cottages had begun to spread along Hall Carr lane, with their crofts and fields at the rear.

The large area which was shown on Yates' map of 1786 as 'Longton Moss' now became usable. The new fields with their regular patterns, so different from the medieval strips around the village itself, are clear to see, and in particular the drainage which created the fields to the south and east of Moss Lane and Gill Lane. Gradually these newer areas became linked, first of all by tracks and footpaths across the countryside, connecting them to the existing roads. Some of these tracks are still clearly visible on the OS map of today, like the one running due south from Marsh Lane across the fields to Meadowhead Lane and on to Hall Carr Lane.

Longton in 1872 appeared to Hewitson[37] 'one of the prettiest in the country. There are numerous small cottages in it; they seem all clean and tidy; many have attached to them little gardens; and the bulk have flowers growing about them.' We have no such

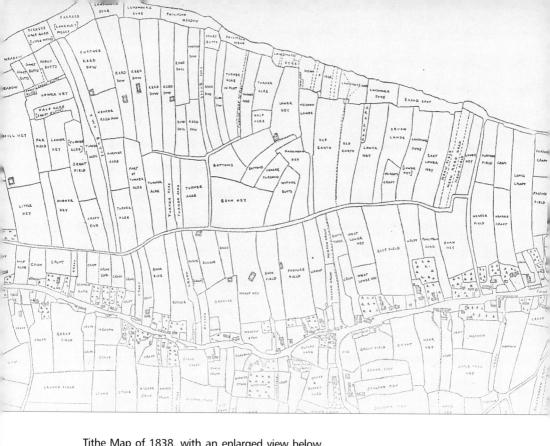

Tithe Map of 1838, with an enlarged view below.

evidence of what the village looked like in 1851, but certainly life was a good deal harder and many living there at that time would not have regarded it as so idyllic. Above all it was a working village, and still retained much of its rural isolation. Contrast this with Penwortham, which by the late 1840s had attracted the well-to-do, anxious to move out of the smoke and noise of over-crowded Preston. Penwortham Hall, originally built for John Horrocks, Penwortham Priory, rebuilt for Lawrence Rawstorne, Hurst Grange, occupied by William Hulton, a barrister and county court judge and Penwortham House, built for George Corry, a Preston cotton merchant, gave Penwortham a new class of wealthy professional residents.[38] It was not until 1881, as we shall see later, that Longton attracted more well-to-do newcomers into the village.

The population of the village had grown rapidly in the early years of the nineteenth century. In 1801 it was 904. It rose to 1340 in 1811, and in 1821 had reached 1791 – a 98% increase in just twenty years. None of the surrounding townships had increased to the same extent. Even Penwortham's population only increased by 43% in the same period.

This increase cannot be explained by the normal increase in births over deaths. Nationally at this time, the average birthrate was in the region of 35–40% of the population. By 1820 the mortality figures had fallen to twenty per thousand, so in normal circumstances one could expect a 'natural' increase of fifteen/twenty births over deaths in every thousand. Longton's population increase is much greater and must have been caused by people moving into the village. This is evident from the histogram – see Figure 1 – produced from the 1821 census figures, where the 'bulge' in men and women in the twenty–forty age group is very obvious. The group explains to some extent the large proportion of youngsters under fifteen, who comprise 44.8% of the total village population. Young married people, both those born in Longton and those migrating into the village, were having more children who were surviving the early years of infancy than had been the case in earlier times.

What brought these newcomers to Longton?

IN THE 1831 CENSUS, 208 were employed in 'trade, manufacture and handicraft', i.e. handloom weaving in this case, and ninety-four in agriculture. It is therefore clear that agricultural work was not the primary attraction. By 1851 this pattern had changed – see Figure 2 – not only in the type of jobs which people had, but in the population size also. By 1851 the total living in the village was 1687, a fall of 5.8%. In Much Hoole, Farington and Croston the opposite happened, and their populations grew steadily between 1821 and 1851, due in part to the development of small textile mills. The pattern of a youthful population in Longton did however remain, for in 1851 39.7% were under fifteen, higher than the national average of 35.2%. The reason for this must lie in the

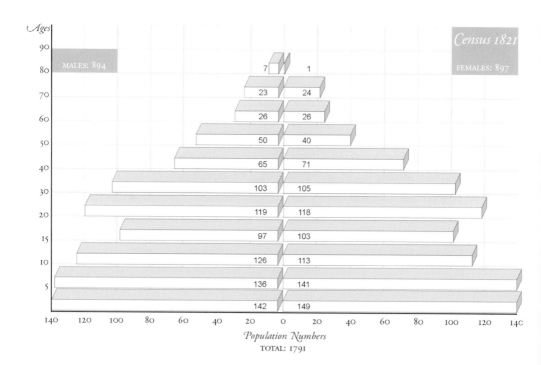

Population Numbers
TOTAL: 1791

increase of 451 between the censuses of 1811 and 1821, who had grown up and married in this ten year period. The age group fifteen to forty-five in 1851 represented 43% of the total, compared with 46% nationally. There was also a drop in the numbers over forty-five years of age – 17% compared with 18.5% nationally. For the same reason that inward migration seemed to account for the population explosion of the earlier years, so migration out of the village can be the only answer for the population fall. A 'natural' decrease through contraception and family limitation cannot be used as an explanation for such methods did not have an appreciable an effect on population in general terms until after the 1870s. In the census of 1841, twenty empty houses are listed and in 1851, eleven, so people were certainly leaving the village. The inevitable reason for the inward and later outward migrations has to lie in handloom weaving. The boom years drew people in from the neighbouring villages, and the effect of the development of the power loom drove them away.

Of the total living in the village in 1851, 64% had been born there, 21% of the new 'migrants' were born within a five mile radius, which included Hutton, Penwortham, Farington, Leyland, Eccleston, Croston, Bretherton and Little and Much Hoole, although in this category the majority came from the nearer villages of Hutton, the Hooles, Bretherton and Leyland. 8% were born in widely scattered parts of the rest of Lancashire. Only two men were born outside the county – one in Berwick-on-Tweed, and the other in Slaidburn, just over the border in Yorkshire. One woman was born in Northamptonshire, one in Leeds and one in Armagh, northern Ireland.

However these figures need to be looked at more closely. Of the 307 households in 1851, eighty-one comprised families where both parents had migrated into the village at some stage, fifty-seven where the father was born outside Longton and forty-one where the mother came from elsewhere. So 58% of households consisted of families where one or both parents had moved into Longton, revealing the considerable migration into the village in previous years when Longton, being a large township compared with the smaller neighbouring villages, was a magnet for those seeking work or to improve their prospects.

In households where both parents were migrants, eight were craftsmen. As we have seen, Mawdsley's the blacksmiths had not been born in the village, and John Clayton, the sawyer, came from Parbold. Edward Moon, a wheelwright, born in Freckleton, had married Margaret from Farington, and had only recently settled in Longton, and James Hefford, a blacksmith, had originated in Rufford and his wife from North Meols. Several of the newcomers had set themselves up as carters, and the rest were farmers (twenty-seven) agricultural labourers (ten) and handloom weavers (twenty-eight). Of the households where the husband was born outside the village, but married a Longton girl, the largest number were weavers, but there was also the same spread of farmers, labourers, dealers and craftsmen. Weaving did not require a large capital outlay and at least until the 1840s it provided a steady income, particularly if the cottage had a small allotment attached which could supply the family with a basic diet. Because Longton was a growing settlement, opportunities existed for craftsmen and dealers alike. In the case of farmers, marrying a local girl gave the opportunity to be on the spot when a tenancy became vacant. William Buck born in Bretherton, and Thurston Hosker from Rufford, who both had farms on Marsh Lane, may well have met their wives while working on local farms before their marriages

Family connections also played a part. John and Elizabeth Fairhurst, both born in Scarisbrick, had a farm on Marsh Lane. William Fairhurst, a weaver, also from Scarisbrick, and John and Robert Fairhurst, although born in Skelmersdale, must have been related, and had also settled in the village.

Numbers 85 and 87 Liverpool Road, originally built in 1850.

Looking at where children were born reveals that some parents had moved from place to place prior to living in Longton. As we have seen, Thomas Pickering, the relieving officer, and Robert Whalley, the police constable, had made several moves during their careers. John Clayton, the sawyer, had made even more. One child had been born in Hesketh Bank, another in Parbold, a third in Newborough and the last in Longton. Job opportunities and changing patterns of employment therefore created a much greater mobility among the workforce than had been the case in previous centuries.

However, among farmers and those owning land, this mobility did not apply. In 44% of households where both partners were born in the village, one sees continuance of surnames which had been part of the village for generations. Families which appeared in parish registers in the seventeenth century were still here in

1851 – Waltons, Mosses, Whittles, Wildings, Beardsworths and Martins. But some of the wealthiest of the seventeenth-century families like the Loxams and Sudells had disappeared, and the fortunes of others had changed considerably. Although the Moss family lived at the Manor House, other branches of the family were by 1851 weavers, small farmers and labourers. Others had diversified. The Blackhursts, who had been blacksmiths for almost two hundred years, and were to be so again, were, in 1851, small farmers and weavers.

Finally, the census enables us to study the sex and age structure of a local community. Before 1801, the study of demography had to rely to a great extent on assumptions made from various scattered sources, and it was therefore difficult for historians to provide an accurate picture of the relationship between the sexes in town and village communities. What has emerged, however, is that up to 1900, there were more boys than girls under the age of twelve, but after that girls predominated, and lived significantly longer than men. However, this imbalance did fluctuate from time to time, and was noticeably greater when wars reduced the young adult male population.

In Longton in 1821, however, there were more girls than boys in the under fifteen age group, although this had levelled out by 1851. Longton differs from the national trend for women to live significantly longer than men. In 1821 there is little difference in the longevity of the sexes, and in 1851, although there were more women in the thirty to forty age group, between the forty to sixty group there were more men than women. Interestingly the mortality rate for the sixty-plus group had reduced, so that in 1821, those living beyond sixty represented 5.9% of the population, and by 1851, it had risen to 7.8%.

The relationship which the enumerator found within each dwelling house which he visited gives us an insight into the family of the past. It is essential, however, to differentiate between the 'household' and the family. A household might well include domestic servants and farm labourers living in. The family unit is more precise. It consisted either of the typical 'nuclear' family of father, mother and children, or the extended family where elderly relatives were included with married sons and daughters and their families.

In Longton in 1851 there were 213 family units of which 164 were nuclear and the rest extended. On average the number of children per family was four. There was no correlation between the occupation of the father and the size of his family. Thus farmers, farm labourers, handloom weavers, innkeepers and shop-keepers showed a similar family size. Although the average number of children was four, some had very large families by today's standards. The Athertons living on School Lane had a family of

Bank Lodge, Liverpool Road. For many years until the 1960s the front room was used by the Midland Bank for its local branch.

nine, ranging from five to twenty-six years. In most families the gap between the arrival of one child and the birth of the next averaged three years.

Up to the 1850s the national average for the age of marriage was 24.6 years for women and 25.7 for men,[39] and figures issued by the Registrar General in 1881[40] of 24.4 years for women and 25.9 for men showed little appreciable change. In Longton in 1851, 59% of the adult population was, or had been, married. It is impossible from the census to know at what age these marriages took place, but of those aged between twenty and twenty-nine, 69% were still single, and of those over thirty, almost one in five remained unmarried, and those who did, appear to have been married later than the national average, judging by the ages of their children. In a study of marriage rates in several parishes in Northants, Lincolnshire, Yorkshire and Nottinghamshire,[41] 48% remained single in the Northants village of Long Buckby in the twenty to twenty-nine age group, and only 11% remained unmarried among those over thirty. In the age group twenty to forty in Longton, when one would expect that the majority had settled into married life, 45% of women and 55% of men were still single.

Naturally, using one particular year i.e. 1851, may give a somewhat false picture, for it cannot be assumed that all of these men and women remained single all their lives. Yet economic uncertainty, lack of job opportunities and suitable housing played an influential part.

Looking in more detail at the men in the twenty to twenty-nine age group who had married, some informed guesses can be made as to why they did so. As we have seen, Thomas Malthus in his *Essay on the Principle of Population* had cautioned 'moral restraint' as a way of achieving one's true fulfilment as a 'rational being'. To people in Longton, still an agricultural community but with a handloom weaving industry in terminal decline, 'moral restraint' was nothing new. Indeed rural villages had for many centuries known what effects a poor harvest would have on their daily lives and almost sub-consciously limited their numbers of children when they knew there would not be enough food to feed them. Young men tended to contemplate marriage only when they could support a family. For example, John Brown (twenty-four) and his wife, Elizabeth, lived with John's parents who kept the Farmers Arms at Whitestake and farmed a hundred acres in the vicinity. John junior already had three children under the age of four years in 1851, but felt his future was assured and indeed he proved to be right, for in 1881, his own son Edward was running the public house. Samuel Wilding (twenty-seven), married to Ann, was a tailor, and with a trade at his fingertips could look forward to a steady economic future. William Riding (twenty) was even more perspicacious. He had married Ann Jump, twelve years his senior. Ann's sister, Cicely, kept the village grocer's shop, and Ann and William lived with her. So William not only had his skill as a bricklayer, but also a roof over his head and a sister-in-law with a thriving shop. Indeed by 1865, Ann Riding had taken over the shop. John Higham (twenty), lived and worked at Whitestake as an agricultural labourer. Other members of the Higham family lived in the area, farming thirty acres and running a cartage business, so he too had the confidence that he could provide for himself and his wife.

Whether some of the other young married men could be so sure of a stable future is questionable. Malthus admitted that it required 'some courage' to refrain from marriage, and the following cases may prove that not all had that restraint. Several were handloom weavers, and some had moved into Longton from the nearby villages of Much Hoole and Bretherton, and by 1851 were faced with working in a trade which was in certain decline, but were loath to move again to face an uncertain future.

Economic pressure was a strong factor in delaying marriage,
but what were the factors, if any, for one in five of those over
thirty to remain single?

FAMILY INFLUENCE played a considerable part. Longton was still
predominantly an agricultural community in 1851. Farms were
small compared with those in southern England, but each family
member had his or her job within the family unit. Farmers' sons
and daughters realised that marriage could increase that unit,
putting more pressure on the limited resources of the land. Marriage
therefore involved the search for another smallholding to rent or
buy, and this was not always easy. It also meant finding a marriage
partner who was prepared to follow such a way of life. For some,
these decisions did not arise. The death of a father or mother in
a farming family meant that sons and daughters took on increased
responsibilities, and marriage became of secondary importance. In
such cases, bachelorhood and spinsterhood seem to have been
inevitable.

Unmarried sons and daughters had little opportunity to find
work outside the home in 1851. Agricultural work, combined with
handloom weaving, meant that the family was an economic as
well as a social unit. The family worked together, had its meals
together and found its recreation in the immediate neighbourhood.
Even those employed in skilled crafts carried on their work at, or
adjacent to, the family home. Only among the labouring classes
was work separated from home, and as a result their children,
often of necessity, had to leave to find a living either as farm
workers living in or as domestic servants. Such living-in employees
were often born many miles from Longton and they frequently
remained single. Their free time was very limited, giving them
little opportunity to make friends or lasting relationships leading
to marriage.

What happened to those who did marry, but through the death of a partner were left as widows or widowers?

IN 1851, there were thirty-four widows – twenty-two of whom were over sixty years of age – and forty-one widowers, twenty-four over the age of sixty. In one or two cases, they had married a second time, but in forty-nine cases the widow or widower was living with a married son or daughter and their children in an 'extended family'. In most of these cases, the elderly relative was listed as 'head of household' and in this way, the family hierarchy remained strong. However, where a wife's parent was part of the extended family, the situation was very different, and the elderly relative was listed as a dependant, and presumably had no financial stake in the family home. For example, Mrs Ellen Norris (seventy-one) lived with her married daughter, Margaret Bamford, at a small farm on Chapel Lane, and did the housework, whereas Edward Martin (eighty-one) lived with his son and family on Marsh Lane farming eighty-five acres, and remained 'head of household'.

But not all widows and widowers lived with their married children, although they frequently lived close by.

It is clear therefore that in a large majority of cases, whether as young marrieds, widowed or single, the family played a very important part, providing mutual support and security. Unmarried brothers and sisters lived together sharing work and domestic duties between themselves. The Spencers, all single – Robert, Richard and John – lived together on Liverpool Road working as handloom weavers, while their sister, Elizabeth, kept house. Margaret Wilding, a spinster, ran a smallholding on Marsh Lane, while her bachelor brother was a weaver and her unmarried sister kept house and did dressmaking.

Family members helped one another if misfortune struck. John Wilding and his wife Mary lived in one of the Old Workhouse

Cottages. They had an infant son and Mary looked after another child called Thomas Spencer, who was the son of John Spencer, a widower living in a cottage next door. It is obvious that John Spencer and Mary Wilding were brother and sister and that John's wife had probably recently died in childbirth.

Job opportunities often occurred through the family. John Lambert was a saddler and living wth him was his nephew Joseph, aged six. John and his wife had no children of their own and possibly Joseph's parents had died, or it was intended that he should be apprenticed to his uncle. Similarly, Henry Hale the shoemaker on Liverpool Road had his widowed son John and his family living with him, as well as Henry Cuddick, his bachelor nephew, who was a journeyman shoemaker.

Families also rallied round if an unwanted pregnancy occurred. Illegitimacy was deplored, yet it was a fact of life, and had to be dealt with. Although the number of illegitimate births was not high in the early Victorian period, representing about 7% of all live births, it fell to about 4% by the end of the century. It is apparent, however, that the births of illegitimate children were not always registered, even after the 1836 Registration Act, and that indeed there may have been concealment of the birth.

In 1851, the Longton census shows that this concealment persisted. The enumerator was not required to list whether a child was illegitimate, and on occasions a 'grandchild' was obviously the child of an unmarried daughter living at home. In one case, a child was entered as 'son of' of an unmarried daughter, and this was crossed out and changed to 'grandson'. This looked better on the official census form, at least from the family's point of view. In all there appear to have been twenty-three cases of illegitimate children at this time.

The baptism register for Longton Chapel between 1847 and 1850 reveals twenty-one entries of children born to spinsters living in Longton and some of them are listed in the 1851 census. Janet

Hindle (twenty-one) had a daughter, Alice, baptised in April 1849, and they were living with Janet's grandparents in 1851, although Alice is listed as 'granddaughter' rather than great-granddaughter. Jane Blackhurst (thirty) and her daughter Margaret, baptised in July 1849, were also living with Jane's widowed grandfather on Marsh Lane, in 1851, and Betty Riding (thirty) lived alone on School Lane with her son aged three, baptised in March 1848.

CHAPTER FIVE

What the Census Revealed

O CCUPATIONS, the sexes, marriages and the family. The 1851 census helps us to find out who lived where, but it can also reveal what jobs people did, how large the family was, where people came from and whether it was a young or ageing population.

The census divided Longton township into four districts. Two of these comprised the old village settlement itself, bounded by Hutton Brook in the north, Meadowhead and Drumacre Lanes to the south and Moss Lane to the east. The other two districts consisted of Hall Green, Hall Carr Lane, Walmer Bridge and Whitestake. These divisions are important and affected to some extent the jobs which people did.

If we look at the male occupations first, in 1851 in the township as a whole 263 men and boys were engaged in farming either as farmers, farmers' sons or agricultural labourers, some 43% of the male population over fourteen years of age. A total of 230 men and boys were employed in handloom weaving, 38% of the same group. In the two areas of the older village settlement, 129 were in agriculture but 132 were weavers, compared with 131 in agriculture and ninety-eight weavers in the Walmer Bridge areas. The higher numbers in agriculture in the latter area can be explained because here the land was drained and brought into cultivation much later than in the central village settlement. This gave the ambitious and the newcomers an opportunity to obtain land and set up as small farmers, whereas land in and around Longton itself had been cultivated and passed down to succeeding generations, giving less opportunity for those who were not established families to buy or tenant land.

The rest of the male labour force, 18%, was engaged in skilled crafts, shopkeeping, brewing and miscellaneous service jobs.

Skilled workers covered a wide variety of crafts – blacksmiths, tailors, shoemakers, sawyers, saddlers, butchers and wheelwrights. There were seven blacksmiths, of which the Mawdsleys are the most well-known in the village. Richard Mawdsley, who ran his own business from the smithy near the Ram's Head, had six children, the eldest, Thomas, being apprenticed to his father. There was also another apprentice, William Cross, who was Mrs Mawdsley's son by a previous marriage. Richard had been born in Euxton, but must have come to Longton in the late 1820s, for his eldest daughter had been born here. There were eleven wheelwrights and their apprentices, which is not surprising at a time when the horse and cart was the essential means of transportation for every rural community.

Before the days of mass-produced clothing, local tailors and shoemakers were a vital part of a village community. Henry Sutton was a master tailor with his workshop near the old mill on Liverpool Road. Henry had been born in Little Hoole and had a large family, for his wife, Margaret, had two children by a former marriage, in addition to their own five children. Henry Hale on Liverpool Road and Ralph Sumner on Marsh Lane were both shoemakers, while Robert Riley near the Black Bull Inn was a master clogger. There were also three brick 'setters' and four carpenters. Thomas Rawcliffe had a flourishing house carpentry business and employed six men and two apprentices. John Holding, who lodged at the Golden Ball, was a sawyer, as was John Clayton, living on Garstang's Row, and both were 'outsiders', being born

in Garstang and Parbold respectively. Thomas Taylor was also a sawyer. His widowed mother lived at Longton Hall Farm, with its 128 acres, and her two eldest sons and a labourer ran the farm. Thomas was married, but his wife is not listed in the census and it may be that she was away and Thomas was temporarily staying at the farm, perhaps doing some work for his mother.

John Lambert, born in Pilling and living on the turnpike road, was a journeyman saddler. John Wignall on Garstang's Row and Richard Wilding of Whitestake were both butchers. Thomas Atherton living on Chapel Lane was a master pipe-maker. Whether he made clay pipes for smoking or clay land-drainage pipes is not made clear by the enumerator. He employed his two nephews Henry and James as apprentices, and, as they both came from a large family of eight children, probably welcomed the opportunity to learn a trade with their bachelor uncle.

There were several carters, two of whom were employed by the Wilkins brewers for their beer deliveries. The rest, who all lived in the New Longton area, were presumably self-employed, and probably carried a variety of goods, although Henry Bennett was specifically a coal dealer.

John Banister, living on Hall Lane, and Robert Sutton of Whitestake, were both gamekeepers, but there is no indication as to where they were employed. John Oxendale, aged sixteen, was a 'stonebreaker' and lived on Hall Carr Lane. Stonebreaking was a solitary and tedious job, which consisted of picking up stones from the ploughed fields, breaking them up where necessary and collecting them for future use on road repairs. It was normally a job for a child, and it may be that John Oxendale was not very bright, although his meagre wage would have helped when his father, who had four other children, had only a labourer's wage.

Opposite: The Black Bull, Liverpool Road, with its unusual overhanging late-Georgian window.

As we saw in the last chapter, in 1851 Longton was very much a working village, and had not developed sufficiently to attract a middle-class professional element. There was no doctor, and the only member of the legal profession was Peter Dawson, son of Henry Dawson of White Cottage on Chapel Lane. He was a solicitor's articled clerk and probably worked in Preston. Jonah Nicholson was the curate at Longton Chapel, although in 1852 he was replaced by the Rev. Lawrence Preston, who remained in the post until 1869. Robert Wilding was the headmaster of Longton Free School; the part played by religion and education in the life of the village is considered in a later chapter. He lived on Marsh Lane in the old school established by the Moss Charity, which had closed by 1851, and the building converted into a dwelling house. John Taylor, also a schoolmaster, lived near Longton Chapel, but whether he taught at Hutton Grammar School or assisted at the nearby Free School is not clear. James Hesketh, who lived with his parents at their farm on Chapel Lane, was also a schoolmaster and taught at Howick School.

By 1851 brewing and malting was a thriving business, dominated by the Wilkins and the Pyes, and both concerns provided work locally. Richard and William Wilkins each employed six men, in addition to members of the family John and James Wilkins who ran the Golden Ball and the Ram's Head respectively. Nevertheless, both concerns had secondary interests for William Wilkins farmed forty acres and James Pye fifty-five acres.

All the public houses which we know today were selling beer in 1851. The evils of drink among the working classes both in town and country had been a cause for public debate ever since the passing of the Beer Act in 1830. This enabled any ratepayer, who paid an annual duty of two guineas, to obtain a licence to sell beer on or off his premises. Spirits, however, could only be bought at a limited number of public houses licensed by the local magistrates.[42]

Drinking in public houses and beer houses was the main social activity of the working classes, especially men. Churches and chapels catered to some extent for the recreation of women and children. For men, the pub and beer house were the only meeting places after a day of hard physical toil, away from their homes which were over-crowded and offered few comforts. Portable bottled beers were not developed for sale until the 1890s. The rise of the temperance movement in 1834, spear-headed by Joseph Livesey, the Preston plasterer who coined the word 'teetotal', was largely Non-Conformist in its beginnings. Yet it had class overtones, for the Victorian middle class, while deploring the 'demon drink' among the working classes, could see nothing wrong with wine drinking in their own homes. Drink was certainly a serious problem. Many families, while having an ostensibly adequate income, were spending unwisely on beer for the husband, and gin for the wife. Seebohm Rowntree's study of poverty in York in 1901 revealed that as much as 28% of the city's working class came into this category.

Legislation in 1872 and later in 1916 regulated Sunday drinking and statutory weekday closing times in public houses, and gradually the problems of drink became less acute. Nevertheless, for many working-class people, the pub remained their principal meeting place and provided friendship, gossip, political debate and often entertainment. The middle classes, at least in the towns, had their own meeting places in private establishments, masonic and rotary clubs, theatres, concert halls and assembly rooms.

It is interesting to speculate on the attitude to drink in Longton. It was thought that the Beer Act in abolishing the duty on beer would reduce public demand for spirits and encourage the sale of beer, which was regarded as more healthy and wholesome. This must have pleased James Pye and Thomas Wilkins, and certainly increased the demand for their locally produced ale. But the temperance movement and the attitude of the Methodists may

The Golden Ball, first tenanted by James Pye, but taken over by the Wilkins family in 1851.

have been a source of considerable irritation to them. The Wilkins family had donated land on Marsh Lane on which the Wesleyan Chapel was built, and were regular worshippers there. However, the story is told that a visiting preacher so incensed Mr Wilkins by preaching hell-fire to those who indulged in drink, that he and his family left the chapel and thereafter attended the Anglican church. For the local labourer a visit to any of the local public houses offered warmth, gossip and friendship. The Golden Ball provided accommodation and an opportunity for the local men to get into conversation with those lodging there, who doubtless had stories to tell. A stroll to the Dolphin, kept by William Buck, appealed to those who liked its remoteness and its proximity to the Marsh, much as they do today.

Thomas Pickering was the relieving officer who administered outdoor relief to the poor and needy in the village. He was not a local man. Born at Whittingham, and his wife at Urswick near

Ulverston, they had lived both in Preston and Tockholes near Darwen before coming to Longton.

The Poor Law Amendment Act of 1834 had seen the closure of the old small parish workhouses and the removal of their inmates to larger establishments, but the system of out-door relief to the able-bodied continued. Penwortham's workhouse had been opened in 1796 on what is now Greenbank Road at Middleforth. It continued to be used as a hostel for elderly male paupers, as an emergency centre for victims of the Preston typhoid epidemic and between 1851 and the early 1860s, when it was finally closed, to house and educate young girl paupers. It was subsequently converted into cottages and renamed Manor Cottages.[43] Longton had established its own workhouse in 1821 where 'Rydal Mount', Liverpool Road, now stands. It consisted of two floors, with kitchen, pantry and dining room on the ground floor, and bed-rooms for the paupers and governor above. The cellar accommodated twenty-four pairs of handlooms.[44]

The day-to-day administration of the workhouse is very well documented in the Overseers' Accounts which cover the period from 1836 to 1839.[45] Men who were fit to work were hired out on a variety of jobs suitable for their age and abilities, and women to work as charwomen or to help in the fields at harvest-time. Children were taught to spin and weave, and any inmate who could read was expected to teach the children their letters and to read and spell. The hours of work were long. In summer the paupers were woken at 5.30 a.m. and worked until 7.00 p.m. with three short breaks for breakfast, dinner and supper. In winter the hours were 7.00 a.m. to 8.00 p.m. At nine o'clock each evening the governor locked them into their bedrooms and they were not allowed to have a candle or to smoke, for fear of starting a fire. Good Friday and Christmas Day were holidays, and although no work was done on Sundays, church attendance was compulsory. Failure to comply with the rules resulted in being 'confined' by

the governor or in reduced meals. Paupers from Much Hoole and
Tarleton were also housed at Longton workhouse. It finally closed
in 1839 and, like Penwortham, the building was converted into
cottages, and shown on the 1851 census as occupied by five families,
all handloom weavers.

After 1834, the former Overseers of the Poor were replaced by
the Poor Law Guardians. In reality, their job was the same. They
appointed the local relieving officer, but largely 'rubber-stamped'
the payment of out-door relief, and authorised the accounts.
Thomas Pickering had to assess local claims and pay eligible
claimants, and in 1851, there were twenty-one paupers who were
receiving relief – fourteen men and seven women, all but three
of whom were weavers.

For many of them, life must have been very hard indeed. Joseph
Leyland, aged sixty-six, 'a former handloom weaver', living with his
wife in a cottage near the Red Lion, was obviously unable to work
and totally dependent upon relief payments. Next door to him lived
Peter Eastham aged twenty-eight. His wife had died, leaving him
with four step-children, and although the eldest worked with his
step-father as a weaver, Peter must have found it a considerable
struggle to feed and clothe the three youngest children, particularly
when handloom weaving was in serious decline, as it was by 1851.
Roger Cross (thirty-eight) and his wife lived at Garstang House and
were also pauper weavers. They had five children all under twelve.
The eldest helped as a bobbin-winder, and a nine-year-old girl
looked after the baby who was a month old. Having several children
who were too young to contribute to the family income was a real
problem, particularly with handloom weaving facing machine competition. Henry Bamford (seventy-four) was a pauper agricultural
labourer. He and his wife looked after their twin grandsons aged
eleven, who were at school, and Henry must, at his age, have found
it well-nigh impossible to find any regular work. Alice Harrison
(seventy-nine) of 16 Garstang's Row was also on poor relief. Her

bachelor son, a weaver, lived with her as did her granddaughter, Jane, who earned what she could as a charwoman to help keep her illegitimate son. Betty Wilson (seventy-eight) who lived at Moorside was also a pauper, for what she could earn by doing a little sewing and running errands for her neighbours was obviously insufficient.

The question of whether claimants for relief were 'deserving' poor seems justified in the above cases. In others, however, questions may well have been asked. Joseph Parker (forty-seven) and his wife Nanny, had eight children. The three eldest were weavers like their father, while the five youngest were at school or at home, and it might be argued that the parents should have thought of the problems of feeding and clothing so large a family.

Robert Whalley was the local police constable living at the police station near where today's Booth's supermarket now stands. Like the relieving officer, Robert Whalley was not a local man. He and his wife had been born in Kirkham, and had subsequently lived at Wrightington and Brindle before coming to Longton. Up to 1840, enforcing the law in rural areas was largely the duty of the unpaid parish constable, who dealt with offences such as poaching, vagrancy, supervising public houses and ale-shops and dealing with drunkenness.[46] But the rapid increase in population, unrest in the factories and agitation against the Poor Law had involved the frequent use of the army to enforce order, at least in the towns.

Between 1801 and 1851, Lancashire's population had increased two hundred-fold and with it came an alarming escalation of crime. In 1836, for example, there were 2,568 convictions for serious offences, largely theft. Preston had set up its own police force in 1815, but many other boroughs had not, and in 1839 the County Police Act was passed, followed in 1840 by further legislation to include the rural areas. This was not before time, for in a letter dated 15 February 1840, a Longton resident wrote to the editor of

the *Preston Chronicle*,[47] complaining that the local younger generation seemed 'to have gratification only in the exercise of turbulent,
unnatural and malignant dispositions', and 'midnight work of
plunders, burglars and wanton and maliciously disposed persons'
made him fearful of staying in the village. In reply, the editor
assured him that 'the labours of the rural police will shortly
commence in your neighbourhood'.

By 1841, some 660 constables and officers had been appointed
in the county as a whole, but at first, discipline among the newly
recruited force was a considerable problem, not the least of which
was being drunk on duty, and many of these early recruits resigned
or were dismissed. In 1844, the constables were equipped with a
dark green uniform and a top hat. They were paid between 16s.
and 18s. a week depending on responsibility. At first there was
considerable resentment against the new rural police constables.
Many thought they were too oppressive, and others regarded them
as an unnecessary expense, for local ratepayers had to bear the
cost of their provision. It was not until 1856 that the Government
agreed to contribute half of the cost of each county's police force.
Petty theft was the major source of crime in rural areas, and
compared with today sentences were harsh, usually several months'
imprisonment with hard labour, or even transportation if it was
not a first offence. Although local rural constables were strictly
disciplined and had to attend church on Sundays, the life offered
attractions to the right man who would otherwise have had little
choice but agricultural labouring.

Looking now at women's occupations in the census, 215 women
aged fifteen and over were working. This represents 26% of the
local population, and is low compared with 47% for Lancashire
as a whole. The remaining 265 were mostly married women
and classed as 'farmer's wife' or 'weaver's wife'. Although they
regarded themselves as primarily wives and mothers occupied
mainly with household tasks, they must have helped on the

farm at busy times of the farming year, or done handloom weaving in their spare time.

The largest number of those working (140) were weavers. Some married women regarded this as their main occupation while their daughters kept house. Others, either older, single girls or widows, found that the money they earned by weaving was helping the family income, or in the case of widows, was their only source of income. Alice Gardner of Pipe house, Drumacre Lane, was aged seventy and still helped her husband to weave.

Forty-one were domestic servants, mostly living in with their employer's family, and these were young single girls. Most of them worked at the local inns or at the larger private houses, and some of them were women born outside Longton. Rose O'Hair (twenty-four) was born in Armagh, Northern Ireland and worked as a domestic servant for Mrs Mary Taylor at Longton Hall Farm. Arthur Dawson living at Grove Cottage employed Ann Molyneaux (forty-four) from Leyland as his housekeeper. Robert Harrison, who lived at Loxhams on Liverpool Road, had Ann Lathom (nineteen) as a house servant. Born at Tarleton, she may have had an earlier connection with Robert Harrison who came from Much Hoole. 'Getting a place' in domestic service frequently came about by hearing of a vacancy from family or friends or from local gossip, often on the part of the girl's mother. A number of Longton girls worked for neighbours or relatives. William Mee of Hall Green employed Mary Sharrock (seventeen) who was doubtless the daughter of John and Mary Sharrock who had an adjacent smallholding, and Edward Martin, also of Hall Green, employed his niece Alice (twenty-one) as a house servant. Mary Bannister (seventeen) worked for the brewer, William Wilkins. Her brother also lived in and worked as a carter, and it is very likely that Margaret Bannister (nineteen) who was employed by Mrs Sarah Moss was of the same family. In all probability these posts came about through personal recommendation.

Although my analysis of women's employment deals with those of fifteen years and over there were quite a number of younger girls who were domestic servants. Mary Hunter, aged only seven, lived in at the Longton Arms, and although born in Penwortham she must have been frequently lonely and homesick.

In large households, domestic servants had their clearly defined duties, be it as housekeeper, cook, housemaid or laundry maid. But in smaller establishments, as in Longton, the servant was in effect 'maid of all work'. This would involve cleaning, laundry, cooking, lighting fires and carrying coals, often from 6.30 in the morning until the family retired to bed. In some instances, the distinction between servant and employer was very marked, to the extent of dictating what they should wear, both indoors and out, and church attendance was often obligatory. Wages, which were usually paid quarterly, or half-yearly, varied widely, depending on the type of work, age and experience and on the geographical area.[48] Nevertheless close links were frequently forged between servants and the families they worked for, which often endured for many years. There is no evidence as to what sort of life these women and girls led in the village in 1851.

The jobs which the remaining thirty-four did covered a wide range. Cicely Jump, together with her married sister Ann Riding, of course, kept the grocer's shop in the village centre, and Mrs Margaret Rawcliffe also had a shop at the end of School Lane. Emma Sutton, a widow, ran a baker's shop on Marsh Lane. It is suggested that shopkeeping was an 'acceptable' occupation for women, especially among skilled workers, and a way of achieving social mobility.[49] Certainly such local shops provided nutritious food and welcome additions to the diet of many families, particularly those where the wife was busy on the farm or engaged in weaving.

Three women worked as charwomen for many households who could not afford live-in servants, and could offer heavier cleaning work to needy women. Elizabeth Rawcliff (twenty-eight) who lodged at a cottage near the police station, was unmarried, and with two small children and the rent to pay, work as a charwoman must have been a hard necessity.

There were others too, at the lowest level of the social scale, who were living on or below the poverty line. Esther Whittle (one) on Garstang Row went out rag-gathering to eker out her husband's wage as a weaver.

At quite a different level were the women who worked as dressmakers and seamstresses. In 1851 there were no dress shops in Longton, and although there were ladies' outfitters in Preston, many better-off women and their daughters had their clothes made personally to order from illustrations and designs in the popular magazines. For girls and women with a talent for sewing and tailoring, this was an attractive occupation and an opportunity to widen one's social horizon. Ann Waring (thirty-five) lived with her very elderly parents who had a smallholding on Marsh Lane. Being single, dressmaking offered just such an opportunity. Mrs Charlotte Taylor (thirty-seven) was listed on the census as a 'visitor' staying with Mrs Mary Moss, a young, quite well-to-do widow on Chapel Lane. It was not uncommon for a regular customer to engage her dressmaker to stay while fittings and alterations were made.

Other aspects of fashion were also catered for. Alice Cunliffe, living at the corner of School Lane, was a straw bonnet maker. In mid-Victorian times, women, young and old alike, wore bonnets, not only for social occasions, but when outdoors in the garden or field for a sun-tanned complexion was regarded not only as unfashionable but un-genteel. Equally essential was Margaret Wilding's job. Aged eighteen, she lived with her parents on Marsh Lane and worked as a stay-maker. After the Napoleonic Wars, the high-waisted loose-fitting gown gave way to tight-waisted dresses and it was every young woman's aim to have an eighteen-inch waist even if it had to be contrived by wearing stays. They were made to measure, using whalebone stitched into a linen corset and were worn by women of all age groups. Margaret Wilding therefore provided an essential yet discreet service for her customers.

Eleven women were farmers. Some were carrying on their late husband's holding, and others were unmarried but running an inherited family farm. Mrs Mary Taylor (sixty-four) and widowed, farmed 128 acres at Longton Hall Farm off Chapel Lane, the largest holding in the village. She had two unmarried sons and a daughter to help. Mrs Ann Park (fifty-seven) single, farmed sixteen acres at Park Farm, Marsh Lane with the help of a labourer who lived in. Mrs Ann Taylor (eighty-seven) also farmed thirteen acres on Marsh Lane and although her married children managed the holding, she is classed as 'head of household'. In common with many cases where control of land was concerned, the 'head of household' of whatever age or sex kept a strict hold on their family status. This is particularly so in the case of Ellen Beardsworth (seventy-eight) with her smallholding of four acres on Marsh Lane. She had four unmarried sons and daughters all living at home, but the sons are classified as 'farm labourers'.

CHAPTER SIX

"Swifter than a weaver's shuttle"

T HE HISTORY of the spectacular growth of the domestic cotton textile industry in Lancashire is fascinating.

Before 1770, certainly in Longton, mainly linen and a little woollen cloth was produced. Women and children did the spinning, and the men the weaving. At that time, a spinning wheel cost a shilling or so, and a loom between six and twelve shillings, so costs were small.[50] The flaw in the domestic system, as far as the local handloom weaver was concerned, was the supply of yarn and his total dependence upon the fluctuations of the market for the sale of his cloth. With the growth of imports and improved communications, the substitution of cotton for linen gradually transformed all aspects of the Lancashire textile industry. Eden in his *State of the Poor* observes that 'all the small farms in Walton, Penwortham and the adjoining country places were weaving farms, having a [work] shop attached to hold a certain number of looms'.

Spinning was the first textile process to be mechanised. This provided the handloom weaver with a plentiful supply of yarn, and enabled weaving to remain a cottage-based industry into the 1840s and beyond in some areas of Lancashire. It was for this reason that John Horrocks came to Preston in 1791, setting up a small workshop in Turk's Head Court just off Stanley Street. He built his first spinning mill, the so-called 'Yellow Factory', in 1792 followed by Moss Mill near Fylde Road in 1796 and Frenchwood in 1797.[51]

Although the development of mechanisation to spinning had been rapid, its application to weaving was delayed. Edmund Cartwright's first power loom of 1785 had many imperfections, and even by the 1820s and 30s the power loom was only suitable for plain fabrics. Handlooms continued to be more reliable for quality goods such as quilted fabric, patterned and figured muslins and mixed yarns.[52]

Entrepreneurs were therefore loath to outlay capital on weaving mills until loom technology improved and there was sufficient inducement to abandon the domestic 'putting-out' system in favour of the power loom. Fluctuations in the market and in particular consumer demand for high quality fabrics were strong inducements to retain handloom weaving, even among major manufacturers such as Horrocks. Even in 1841, only one worker in five was employed in factory industry, which was based in urban rather than rural areas.

Handloom operator.

The old dual economy of handloom weaving and agriculture had long provided for some a very useful addition to the family income, and for others an essential part of their meagre existence. Up to the 1830s, the home trade in cotton goods absorbed a large proportion of the production, with exports going to Europe and America, and in good years the demand for hand-woven cloth remained high. Consequently, the dual economy continued, and attracted to it those who previously worked in agriculture.

Indeed, when demand was high, the handloom weaver could earn more than the power-loom weaver, who traditionally was better paid. Whole families were engaged in weaving, so much so that in 1843, Lawrence Rawstorne referred to the backwardness in farming methods in and around Longton. He attributed this largely to the fact that handloom weaving was so lucrative that it took precedence over any desire to improve agricultural practices.

Timmins' figures [53] from the analysis of parish marriage registers show that in the Penwortham parish (which included Longton) 58% of bridegrooms were handloom weavers, the third highest proportion for the parishes studied in Lancashire.

John Horrocks, having quickly built up his spinning mills, established an extensive 'putting-out' system, based upon strategically placed warehouses within easy reach of Preston. By 1799, he had warehouses in Blackburn, Chorley, Leyland, Darwen, Kirkham, Longridge and in Preston itself.[54] Later in the same year, he also established a warehouse in Longton. Where this was is not known, and surprisingly from the firm's cash books, it only existed from May 1799 until June 1800. This is a considerable mystery. The takings from the Longton warehouse for the months of January to June 1800 amounted to £955 19s. 3d., compared with, for example, the Leyland warehouse, figures for which were £3,276 10s. for the same period. Leyland's population at this time was twice that of Longton, and one could argue that the Longton figures were rather low in consequence. The firm's Croston warehouse takings for August 1802 to May 1803 was £1,590, where the population was almost the same as Longton. If Horrocks had other competition for 'putting-out' in Longton, I have found no evidence of it. However the Horrocks ledgers reveal that a warehouse was set up at Hutton in 1807 which continued to exist until the mid-1830s. Hutton's close proximity to Longton may have offered the firm a new area for development while retaining contact with the Longton 'out-workers'. To add to the mystery, Timmins, in discussing the family income of handloom weavers, cites Thomas Wilding of Longton who, with his wife and two teenage children, earned 28s. 1d (7s. per loom) per week during a thirteen week period in 1835, and was employed by Horrocks of Preston. The takings from the Hutton warehouse were considerable. From October to December 1807 they were £1,309 5s. 9d. and in 1815, from January to June £3,073 8s. 4d. By 1832 however, the figures had dropped to £300. This reflects the development of Horrockses power loom weaving mills, which began in the 1820s and by 1836 had a total of 764 power looms in operation.[55] Inevitably, the rural warehouses were closed, and only those in Preston, Ormskirk and Manchester remained, although the firm did continue some hand weaving until the early 1850s.[56]

By the mid-1830s the demand for finished cloth knew no bounds, not only for the home market, but also for the expanding markets in the Far East. Lancashire textile entrepreneurs began to invest far more of their capital in power looms to meet the demand. But this was to foreshadow the beginning of the end for many handloom weavers, particularly in the major textile towns. In order to maintain fixed costs, factory owners opted to keep their power looms working and laid off their handloom weavers. The typical Lancashire entrepreneur was largely a self-made man. A case study[57] reveals that a large majority were middle class. They had previous experience in the industry, either as partners or in a lesser capacity, and those who set up their own businesses did so either with financial help from their parents, or their own savings. Many went into partnership to share initial costs, and often rented property on a 'room and power' basis until they could afford to buy. Several who were of an inventive turn of mind produced new or improved machinery. Their success depended in part on previous experience, coupled with a degree of luck. Some adopted the Horrocks policy of setting up their own spinning mills, 'putting-out' yarn to domestic weavers and only adopting the power loom later, whereas others established power weaving mills at an early stage.

In Longton, the 'putting-out' system must have applied until the 1850s, as analysis of the 1851 census shows. Working at home on their looms – for I found no evidence of loom shops in Longton – they received their yarn, and in return were paid a wage for the cloth produced. Normally the husband did the weaving and organised the work to be done by the rest of the family, with the younger children and elderly relatives helping to wind the weft. 'Bearing home day' came round each week, when the finished cloth was taken to the 'putter-out' and fresh yarn for the following week was collected. How the Longton weavers were supplied with yarn and who marketed their cloth between 1800 and 1807 when the Horrockses' warehouse had closed and later, after the mid-1830s when the warehouse at Hutton also closed, must remain a mystery. Whether a local weaver acted as agent for Horrocks and regularly supplied yarn and returned the cloth to Preston is not revealed by any documentary evidence.

In Longton in 1851, 38% of working males were handloom weavers, and this equates with Timmins'[58] figures for Hoole and Croston, where, with no local power loom factor, the situation was the same. In contrast, in Penwortham and Leyland, handloom weaving was already declining due to the establishment of local mills. 65% of working women were employed in handloom weaving, although this figure has to be treated with some caution as explained in the last chapter. In Longton 38% of all weavers, both male and female, were in the nineteen to twenty-nine age group, and only 11% were over fifty. These figures are lower than in areas such as Croston and Much Hoole in Timmins' findings, and must be due to the continued reliance on agriculture as an alternative occupation in the Longton area. Nevertheless they do show that young people still remained in handloom weaving even in 1851, primarily due to the influence of family preferences to stay in the industry, despite its impending decline. The continuance of the family working group is particularly notable in two cases. Ellen Walton, living on Chapel Lane, was a widow aged sixty, and her whole family of five daughters and three sons were weavers. Likewise, Henry Knowles (seventy-seven) who lived next door, had his son, daughter-in-law and four grandchildren all working for him.

By 1850 in the large textile towns of Burnley, Blackburn, Oldham, Stockport and Ashton-under-Lyne, the production of coarse fabrics on power looms was pre-eminent, although the weaving of high quality fabrics by handloom served only to delay the inevitable.

Handloom weaving is a classic case of an industry which expanded, fed by its own success, and destroyed itself by its failure to recognise its impending demise.

The production of simple calico cloth was not a skilled trade, indeed 'a lad of fourteen may acquire a sufficient knowledge of it in six weeks'.[59] Compared with agricultural work, weaving was more lucrative. 'Who will work for 1s.6d or 2s.0d a day at a ditch, when he can get 3s.6d to 5s.0d a day in cotton work and be drunk four days out of seven',[60] was a true if somewhat cynical comment. Women and children, who had previously played a minor role in the rural economy, became a significant element in the labour force. Wives, unmarried sisters and daughters, the elderly and older children were involved on an appreciable scale. Even in workhouses, handloom weaving was the main activity provided. The principal attraction, however, was that handloom weaving kept the family together in rural areas at a time when mechanisation was beginning to impact upon urban families. While demand continued to outstrip supply, the domestic weaver was able to maintain a reasonable living. But as competition from the power loom increased, the handloom weaver fell into the inevitable spiral of working longer hours for less money, coupled with the lack of alternative work. Factory work, with its lure of higher wages, appealed to young people, both men and girls. Their parents, physically and mentally less able to adapt to the regime of factory life and the lack of 'community' in the towns, remained behind, hoping to continue in their old ways for as long as they were able.

Much has been written of the misery and suffering of the handloom weavers. The first evidence of their opposition came in 1826 from those parts of Lancashire which were not the old traditional hand weaving areas. Elsewhere the deprivation was very real, but more prolonged and less well-documented. The rural weaver was the victim of market forces over which he had no control. Whereas in the past he could look to his neighbours for advice, and to his community for a consensus of opinion, he was now on his own, and had to decide his own future for good or ill.

The sufferings and privations of Lancashire handloom weavers eventually reached the attention of Parliament. In the 1830s several Parliamentary enquiries took evidence of the effects on their living standards and the decline in their social status. Witnesses who were called to give evidence painted a picture of the golden age of the domestic dual economy and contrasted it with the later realities of low wages, cottages made cheerless by the sale of all but the barest essentials, a diet of little more than oatmeal and potatoes, and above all, the end of a way of life which had given them a place in their local community.

Parliament did not wish to become involved and remained apathetic. Although a Royal Commission was appointed in 1837, its report was not completed until 1841, by which time the plight of the handloom weavers was of lesser importance than the more pressing problem of life in the new industrial towns and the conditions in their factories. In 1845 Engels had written 'the history of the handworkers has been one of continued retreat in face of the machine'. Sadly, the Lancashire handloom weaver was the first victim of technological change, and he had to learn from his own experience that in the end, only he could decide what he should do.

How did people in Longton come to terms with the situation?

THE 1851 CENSUS shows that weaving continued, even then, to provide some sort of a living. While accepting Timmins' findings for the continuance of a proportion of young people in the industry, it is necessary to look at these in more detail. Ultimately, it was the male head of household who had to make the decision as to whether to stay or leave the village. Among the younger married male weavers, only twenty-seven were under thirty-five years of age, whereas those over thirty-five totalled seventy-eight. This would imply that prior to 1851, some of the young marrieds had already left Longton. But such decisions could not have been taken lightly. The census can only give a picture of a family or individual at a particular point in their lives, and the historian has inevitably to make assumptions from this. Nevertheless, one can ask what one would have done in the circumstances.

Take for example the Houghtons, who lived in the centre of Longton in one of the weavers' cottages in Parker's Row. Richard was forty-two and his wife Ellen thirty-three. They had six children. The two eldest, aged thirteen and eleven, were weavers, as were their parents. The younger children were aged seven, five, one, and one month. What should Richard do? Move to

Preston where rents would be higher and where he might have to live in a cellar-dwelling, damp and airless? Could he get a job in a mill which would pay enough, and if his wife had to go out to work, who would look after the youngest children? How would the two eldest take to working long hours in a factory? Richard probably knew that it was far easier for women and children to find jobs than for men. Thomas Hosker aged thirty lived on Marsh Lane, with his wife Sarah and four children aged from six years to six months. He had similar problems. Could he earn enough to support the family, and if not, who would look after the children if his wife had to work too? These were difficult decisions to make.

Added to which, poverty also had a part to play. In the younger age groups two of the households were classed as paupers and in the older age groups there were ten who were paupers.

Henry and Jane Woodcock who lived at Garstang House were twenty-nine and twenty-eight respectively, and both were weavers. They had four children aged from seven years to six months. Both Henry and Jane were listed as paupers, and in all probability on poor relief, paid by the relieving officer, Thomas Pickering, possibly because of some temporary illness or disability. If they moved to Preston could they continue to get outdoor relief, when their case was not known to the authorities, and who might be less sympathetic? If not they would be forced into the workhouse, where the family would immediately be separated. Far better to stay in Longton.

Nevertheless, people had left the village, as has already been shown by the fall in population from its peak in 1821, but this fall had been gradual – 2.6% from 1831 to 1.8% in 1851. This can only be regarded as a trickle rather than haemorrhage. But where did they go? Some clues lie in the Preston census for 1851.

By the 1840s Preston was booming – 'the town was increasing at a very rapid rate, tall chimneys and loom sheds were rising as if by magic'.[61] Although principally concentrating on spinning, most of the newer mills combined spinning with the weaving process, and inevitably they became a magnet for those from the surrounding areas seeking work. The influx of migrants is clearly seen in the town's census returns. From a population of some 6,000 in the eighteenth century it reached a staggering 83,000 by 1861, and in 1851, 50% of the labour force worked in the town's cotton mills. It was therefore likely that those who left Longton gravitated to Preston. I researched the Preston census for 1851, looking for those listed as 'Born in Longton', accepting of course that in most cases it was not possible to discover when they had migrated there. In some cases, however, where their children were born gives a clearer indication. Stephen Wignall, a widower aged forty-two, had four children all of whom had been born in Longton, so he must have left the village after the birth of his youngest child aged seven, i.e. sometime after 1844. Similarly, John Knowles, aged thirty-five, also a power-loom weaver, had four children, three born in Longton, but the youngest, aged two, born in Preston, so he must have left Longton sometime after 1849.

Of the men originally born in Longton, some 50% had gone into the textile industry, mainly as power-loom weavers. Some had become overlookers, piecers or carders, and one or two were tacklers, mechanics, beam carriers and warehousemen. Of the remainder, some had become tradesmen – tailors, journeymen maltsters and plasterers – others had found employment with one or other of the railway companies which developed between 1838 and 1850. One became a gas works stoker, for Preston was one of the earliest towns to develop gas lighting in 1815. Another was employed as a fireman on a dredging machine, presumably working on the Ribble Navigation Channel, begun in 1806 to provide a deeper access to the sea. One or two were drapers, or kept public houses, two were cowkeepers, possibly connected with the cattle market or abattoir. One worked as a groom, another as an ostler at an inn on Fishergate, and father and son were gardeners living on South Meadow Lane. Several were carters and some youngsters found work as errand-boys, and in two cases as french polisher and attorney's clerk. Intriguingly, James Hardman, aged sixty-three, was a 'curer of spinal complaints' at his house on Cross Street. Of the women, almost all were single and lodging in the town, and nearly all were working as power-loom weavers. The others, also single, were employed as servants living in, either in public houses or with private families. One took in washing.

For the majority of men and women who, at some stage in their lives, had left Longton, Preston provided work which they could not have found otherwise, and for others the opportunity to use the skills which they already had. The influence of kinship and community ties among migrant workers in Preston is borne out by the evidence of the 'Longton born' in the 1851 census. On Back Canal Street lived Margaret Beckinson, a widow of sixty-two, with her three unmarried children, all in their twenties, and next door lived another son, Thomas, with his wife and young child. This enabled Thomas's wife Rachel to work as a powerloom weaver, while his mother Margaret and an unmarried sister cared for his three-year-old daughter and the day-to-day running of the two houses. Similarly, Richard Knowles, sixty-one and a blacksmith, lived with his wife on Brunswick Street, together with his married daughter and her husband, who was a brewer.

Contacts with Longton neighbours often helped when lodgings or jobs had to be found. Thomas Garstang, a carter, living with his wife Elizabeth in Castle Inn Yard, had Thomas and Elizabeth Blackhurst lodging with them. The Garstangs and Blackhursts were families which had lived in Longton for several generations, and the village ties thus helped in the transition to the town. Henry Sutton, twenty-five, who was single and worked as a tailor, lodged with Esther Berry, a widow, who was a mangle-keeper. Ths arrangement worked to their mutual advantage, providing

Henry with accommodation and Esther with some additional income. Joseph Bateson, who was an overlooker, may have put in a good word for William Nixon, seventeen, who lodged with him and worked as a cotton-piecer, probably in the same mill. Catherine Wise, twenty-six, and a widow, lived in a house next to St John's Vicarage in Avenham. She had six acres of land and is listed as a 'gardener'. Born in Longton, she employed four men as labourers, two of whom, Richard Heaton and Thomas Mayor, were also from Longton. Richard's two unmarried sisters, Lydia and Helen, were servants to Mrs Wise. Ann Wikins, who ran a public house in Anchor Wiend (now since disappeared), and who must have been related to the Wilkins family who had a thriving brewery business in Longton by 1851, employed Mary Carr as a servant. Aged twenty-six and single, Mary had also been born in Longton.

It was not always possible to use family or local connections to ease the change from village to town life. Parents who wished to arrange work and training for their unmarried daughters were especially anxious to guard them against the possible evil influences of living away from home. They achieved this by finding them positions with respectable families. Hannah Jolly, aged twelve, boarded as a pupil in 'Ladies Millinery' with Miss Elizabeth Carr at 131, Church Street, which must have been a source of some satisfaction to Hannah's father, Thomas Jolly, who ran a grocer's shop on Garstang's Row, Longton. Edward Harrison, attorney and solicitor, who lived with his family on East Cliff, employed two Longton girls, Alice Riding, twenty-two, and Alice Booth, eighteen, as house servants.

For some, however, leaving Longton had been far less successful. Listed as inmates of the Preston workhouse in 1851 were Betty Tattersall, thirty-three and unmarried, with a month-old baby boy, and Alice Knowles, forty-four, also unmarried, with two children aged thirteen and two. Even those who had moved and had made a new life for themselves may have looked back with some nostalgia for their days in Longton. Although many of their cottages had been cramped and often damp, there was space around them and the open fields beyond. In Preston, the working-class housing was either situated in alleyways and courts off the main streets, in back-to-back terraces around the mills near the canal, in the Ladywell and Maudland Bank areas, or eastwards in the streets which grew up bounded by Church Street and Stanley Street where Horrockses had set up the first of their mills.

For those who stayed behind, the village and the work it provided remained much as before. But income from handloom-woven cloth had almost gone. Subsequent censuses show a continuing decline in population in the village. In 1851 it had been 1,687. By 1861, it was 1,637 and in 1871, 1,455. This continued until 1891 when the total was 1,333, and it was not until 1901 that the tide turned and a population of 1,701 was recorded.

Until the opening of Longton Bridge railway station in 1882 and the establishment of Crewdson and Grierson's mill at Walmer Bridge some years earlier, life in the village scarcely changed. Still a primarily agricultural community it continued to be dominated by the seasons and fluctuating weather, as revealed in the local press and the Penwortham parish magazine, which began publication in 1863.

In June 1850 the *Preston Guardian* reported 'Good weather. Promise of good harvests. Wheat, oats, beans forward', but a few days later, 'Thunderstorms and torrential rain affected Preston areas and all East Lancashire'. The parish magazine of 1865 records that 'the village and neighbouring Longton were visited on Monday, 22 May with the most terrific thunderstorm ever witnessed in this locality', and that cattle plague had affected Penwortham, Howick and Hutton during 1865–66. Again on 11 March, 1871, 'Severe earth tremor felt in North and West Lancashire. Occurred about 11 a.m., and lasted 5 seconds. 42 degrees and warm for the time of year.'

Disease, too, was newsworthy, especially when individuals were affected, and there were fears of an epidemic. The parish magazine again: 'Two children died of Asiatic cholera. Their father, John Beardsworth, had been employed on the punts attached to the dredging machine now at work in the channel of the Ribble, near the Naze Point. The only means imaginable by which the disease might have been communicated to him is the water of the Ribble, which the men on the punts are obliged to drink, not having access to any other'. Later: 'Preston Board of Guardians made cholera medicine available, free of charge, at Mr Pickering's house, the Relieving Officer Longton.' Even in February 1895, a press report states, 'Severe weather. The River Ribble has been frozen over for several weeks', and in September 1896 the local harvest festival suffered from 'want of fruit' and 'embattled flowers', due to adverse weather.

Longton, therefore, had managed to survive the worst effects of the death of the handloom, although for some, life must have been a struggle. Until the turn of the century, it remained a rural community, influenced much as it had been for centuries by the weather and the subsequent success or failure of the harvest.

CHAPTER SEVEN

The Changing Scene

ooking again at the village in 1881 when the census of that year was made, it is surprising to find how little Longton had changed in the intervening thirty years. One major difficulty lies in the lack of contemporary maps, which was less of a problem in 1851. The Ordnance Survey carried out a much more detailed and accurate survey of Lancashire between 1888 and 1893, and it

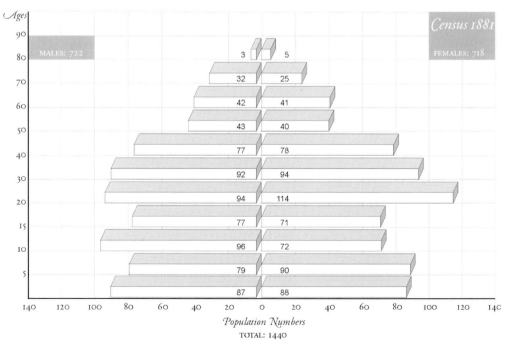

Ages

Census 1881

MALES: 722   FEMALES: 718

Age	Males	Females
80	3	5
70	32	25
60	42	41
50	43	40
40	77	78
30	92	94
20	94	114
15	77	71
10	96	72
5	79	90
	87	88

140 120 100 80 60 40 20 0 20 40 60 80 100 120 140

Population Numbers

TOTAL: 1440

provided superb detail as never before, showing every feature in its correct shape and area. The Longton sheets of 1893, to a scale of twenty-five inches to the mile, do just this, but of course, are twelve years after the census, and therefore in tracing the enumerator's progress certain assumptions have to be made on occasions. Two features were to have a major impact on the village soon after the 1881 census. The opening of the Preston–Southport railway line in 1882 completely changed the local landscape, cutting a deep swathe across what had for many centuries been a completely rural parish. The building of St Andrew's church in 1887 also radically altered the centre of the village itself.

By 1881, Longton had become a more desirable place in which to live, and was attracting a more affluent element. Barrett's trade directory of 1882 mentions New Hall, The Grove, the Mansion House and Chestnut House as 'highly respectable dwellings', and with the trees lining the Liverpool Road, it presented an attractive appearance and a sense of greater well-being.

Once again we follow the enumerator, but this time, we begin at Longton Hall, adjacent to the present-day library. Called Longton New Hall to distinguish it from Longton Hall on Chapel lane, it was built in 1863–64 by Henry Dawson, who in 1851 had lived at White Cottage on Chapel Lane. Next to New Hall was a bricklaying and joinery business run by James Riding, who must have been related to William Riding whose sister-in-law, Cicely Jump, had kept the grocer's shop in 1851. Then came Richard Bradshaw's eight-acre farm and Ann Pickering's shop. Ann was the widow of Thomas Pickering who had been the relieving officer in 1851. Her daughter Harriet was a dressmaker and her son Edward a 'telegraphist/Civil Servant'. Across the road was the smithy where Richard Mawdsley carried on his blacksmith's business. The building still remains today, although is now converted into a private house. The Ram's Head as we know it today bears no resemblance to the imposing Victorian structure which existed in 1881.

The Ram's Head Hotel, Chapel Lane, replaced by a new building.

Opposite the church was a row of cottages occupied by several labourers, and in the area now occupied by the former Booth's store and the telephone exchange was a fifteen-acre farm run by Henry Sumner, which must have been the Parker's Farm of 1851, and two houses occupied by Mrs Margery Frankland (seventy-six) a retired farmer, and Mrs Annie Morgan (fifty) a retired clothier. These properties were demolished, for by 1911, when a further OS map was issued, a pair of brick-built semi-detached houses had been built which, in their turn, I remember being bulldozed down to make way for the telephone exchange in 1977. Beyond these lay the Mansion House which had been built in the 1870s. In 1881, it was occupied by Thomas McGuffog Esq. who was a cotton spinner. In the early years of the century the McGuffogs had owned a linen drapery shop at 163 Friargate, Preston, and by the 1850s owned Murray Street spinning mill. The Mansion House was an imposing dwelling and in 1881 it had stables to the side of the drive. It was demolished in 1999 to make way for the new Booth's supermarket.

The Rev. John Johnson, the vicar, is listed as living at 'the Parsonage', but this cannot be the house we now today as Glebe

Liverpool Road, one hundred years ago, when cattle could be driven through the village undeterrred by motor vehicles.

House for I understand this was not built till after 1900, and I can only assume that the parsonage house mentioned in 1851 still remained. The Rev. Johnson was a widower who lived with his sister Elizabeth and her two children, Mary and William. She must also have been widowed and acted as his housekeeper, assisted by Margery Breakell, a domestic servant. His ministry, which began in 1873, continued until 1905, when frequent bouts of ill-health forced him to resign at the age of sixty-six (the oak lectern in St Andrew's church was purchased in his memory).

At Chestnut House lived Mrs Nancy Taylor (seventy-nine) a retired druggist, together with her elderly sister Mrs May Hawksworth and Thomas Dand their domestic servant. Mrs Taylor's husband John had been in business as a druggist at 157 Friargate, according to a Preston trade directory of 1841. Next door to them was Manor House Farm, occupied in 1881 by Thomas Fairhurst, and beyond that the Manor House where Mrs Sarah Moss

Liverpool Road, Longton. Former Ram's Head (old building) on the left with the churchyard on the right.

(sixty-seven) still continued to live. She and her husband Richard had been living there in 1851, but Sarah was now a widow and her married daughter Hannah Breakell and her grandson Alfred Breakell-Moss lived with her. Alfred, who subsequently inherited the manorial estate of the Moss family, continued live at the Manor House, taking an active part in village life through the Parish Council, St Andrew's church and as a trustee of Hutton Grammar School. In 1881 the Old Parsonage was occupied by Miss Elizabeth Taylor (sixty-one) a 'landed proprietress'. Nearby lived William Tuson who farmed 102 acres, and then came the row of cottages to the east of the Red Lion, built sometime between 1851 and 1881 and occupied by an agricultural labourer and a cellarman who must have worked either at the Red Lion or at the Golden Ball. Peter Hacking, assisted by his wife and daughters, Louisa and Lottie, kept the Red Lion, and the Boltons, with a family of eight children and a lodger, lived at Cobble

Cottage. At the house next to the present-day bridal shop lived Mrs Margery Wilkins (seventy-one), a retired publican; in 1851, she and her husband James had kept the Ram's Head, but by 1881, James had died, and Margery's daughter Mary and a grandson Joseph Tasker lived with her, together with Thomas Tuson, who acted as domestic servant and groom.

At the top of Marsh Lane was Ann Riding's shop. In 1851, Ann and her sister Cicely Jump still ran the grocer's shop, but by 1881, Cicely had died and Ann herself was a widow and had moved her business. In 1865 her shop had been connected to the national telegraph network, and it must have been here that Edward Pickering, the telegraphist mentioned earlier, worked. For many years after Ann Riding's death, her daughter Margot continued to run the grocery shop. In the thirty years since 1851, Marsh Lane had changed little. Ann Harrison did dress-making, James Hogarth made boots and shoes and Henry Walton kept a grocer's shop. Most of the other Marsh Lane inhabitants

Shops along Liverpool Road, Longton.

Shoe shop on Liverpool Road, now a wedding dress shop.

were farmers or farm labourers. The majority of the holdings were of a few acres only, a continuing legacy of the medieval strip farming previously mentioned, between Marsh Lane and Back Lane. The larger units, like those of Thomas Beardsworth (seventy-three acres), and Richard Taylor (seventy acres), were at the lower end of the lane on the later enclosed land. William Fairhurst kept the Dolphin, still referred to in 1881 as a 'beer house', and farmed the twenty-six acres adjacent to it.

Beyond and bounded by the old and new 'sea cop' – the embankment built to withstand the River Ribble's high tides – was the settlement of Hall Green, still in 1881 a somewhat isolated community consisting of the larger farms of Richard Cox, James Rigby, Richard Hesketh and Robert Martin. Hall Carr Lane remained much as it had been in 1851, with its cottages with gardens and crofts to the rear, occupied largely by smallholders, farm labourers and several weavers. A newcomer was John Clitheroe who was employed as a gas maker at the cotton mill, owned by Crewdson and Grierson at Walmer Bridge. The mill offered work for both men and women locally, and was a welcome employer in an area which was still largely agriculturally based. By 1911, however, the gas-making plant had been abandoned and is shown on the OS map of that year as 'defunct gasometer'.

Unlike today, the turnpike road – the old A59 – offered a view of open countryside between Walmer Bridge and School Lane, although Longton Arms, tenanted in 1881 by William Mayor, offered lodging accommodation to three stonemasons who were working on the new railway bridge which spanned the turnpike road and would be open for use the following year. At the corner of Drumacre Lane lived John Ditchfield who farmed a couple of acres and let off part of his house to four Irish navvies and a stonemason from Stranraer in Scotland who were also working on the railway. In 1877, John Ditchfield had been a tailor, but by 1881, and aged seventy, he had obviously retired. There had been considerable changes in School Lane. Arthur Dawson, who had lived at Grove Cottage in 1851, had left. He may have been the younger brother of Henry Dawson at New Hall. The original cottage had been extended and altered to accommodate Richard Wilkins the brewer and his family. The old workhouse, converted into dwellings in 1851, was now occupied by only one family. At the other end of School Lane near the church lived several agricultural labourers, an elderly hawker and Edward Walsh and his wife, who accommodated eight farm labourers originating from County Kerry and from Scotland. Nearby lived Martin Brunton, a blacksmith who probably worked for the Mawdsleys at the smithy, but by 1910, in a trade directory of that year, had set up his own business in the village.

The old Longton chapel and the area around it was to change appreciably within the next six years, when the present St Andrew's church was built in 1887. Raising the money not only to build the new church but to demolish the old chapel and extend the graveyard all took time. In 1881 an application to the Consistory

Court in Manchester to defer the demolition of the old building was made, and there were delays in 1883 to the proposals to stop up Back School Lane, which was to be incorporated into the new graveyard. Not least of the difficulties must have been dealing with the families who, as we have seen, were living in the old properties in Back School Lane. However when the enumerator came to the village in 1881, they must have been largely removed, for he notes 'three uninhabited houses' on the site.

Returning to the centre of the village, the church Sunday school on the site of the present church hall had replaced an early building, and it served both as a Sunday school and as a day school on weekdays. This arrangement continued until 1925, when the County Primary School, later to become the Infants School, was built on School Lane. Subsequently the infant children were absorbed into the newer Longton Primary School across the road, and the old school was demolished in 1998. Beyond the Sunday school on Liverpool Road were two cottages occupied in 1881 by a bricklayer's labourer and a coachman, and although both were later considerably extended, their origins are still visible. Further along the road lived William Marsden, the police constable, with his wife and family, George Pritt, the grocer, and Henry Hale who had retired from his shoe-making business. Between them and the Black Bull was a small farm occupied by James Lyons where Holme Lea now stands. It must be remembered that the houses on Pinfold were not built until the 1960s and the terrace of houses, numbers 101 to 111, Alderley and The Drive and the two shops near the Black Bull, were gradually built after the turn of the century.

John Mayor was the licensee at the Black Bull, and the brother of William who kept the Longton Arms. Nearby lived Mrs Sarah Taylor, an elderly widow of independent means, and beyond her house was a stretch of open fields. Opposite Orchard Lane stood Holme Farm, occupied in 1881 by Mrs Alice Whittle (seventy-eight)

Marsh Lane. Lantern Cottage (bottom picture) was formerly a house and grocer's shop combined. A blacksmith originally lived next door at Bury's Cottage who employed two girls and a young man as domestic and farm servants. I am told that in the early 1900s the farm was bought by the Wilkins family, who employed a farm bailiff. Each morning the family's gardener was sent across the field path from The Grove to collect the day's supply of milk, eggs, cream and butter. The butter was made into small pats each stamped with the initial 'W'. Next to the farm stood three cottages which still exist today, as an off-licence, a newsagent's and a solicitor's office. In 1881 two were occupied by agricultural labourers and the third by John Johnson and his family of nine children. He was a tailor and also ran the village post office. He was still in business in 1910. Open fields separated these cottages from William Sutton's house and tailor's workshop at the rear. William's father Henry had been in business in 1851, but by 1881 the firm had expanded and employed three men and two boys. The nearby windmill and its adjacent house, which had been a thriving business owned by Thomas Barron in 1851, is not referred to in the 1881 census. Certainly nobody seems to have been living at the mill house, although in 1910 Richard Roskell occupied the house and delivered soap, household goods and paraffin lamp oil by cart, using the ground floor of the mill as a store. The old mill was demolished and new houses built.

Across the road and opposite The Grove was Dobson's farm and the row of cottages nearby, which remain just as they were in 1851. However, The Hillock, now Hillock filling station, must have been built sometime between 1851 and 1881, and Philip Howard, who was an agent for agricultural fertilisers, lived there at the time of the 1881 census. Little had changed around the Golden Ball. The adjacent cottages were occupied by a farm labourer, a brewer's labourer and Mrs Ada Wilkins, a widow of forty-eight. The Golden Ball, kept by Richard Harrison who was helped by his three young daughters, sold not only beers and spirits, but also provided accommodation, for four labourers were lodging there on census day.

Beyond the village, little had changed. It is hard to visualise the area which lies between Longton and New Longton as it must have been before the A59 by-pass was built. But in 1881 it was open countryside, with only scattered farmsteads. Houses and smallholdings had begun to grow up along Gill Lane, but New Longton was still undeveloped and consisted of rather isolated groups of cottages and small farms on the edge of what we know as New Longton proper. A school had been built on the present site in 1857, but it was not until the opening of the station that the area began to develop apace. Many of the older late Victorian houses built on Chapel Lane and Station Road are clear evidence of the impact which the railway had.

CHAPTER EIGHT

Another Census

By 1881 male occupations had changed radically. Handloom weaving had gone, and other jobs had taken its place. There were 272 men and boys working in agriculture, either as farmers, farmers' sons, or labourers and farm servants, slightly more than had been engaged in farming in 1851. This was contrary to the national trend, where the drift away from the land was inexorable, and by 1900 those who lived and worked on the land were in a minority. The increased use of machinery for harvesting and threshing had replaced the need for hand labour. Many farmers were in financial difficulties and after the 1880s the acreage of land under cultivation had decreased as small farmers sold up and left the countryside. On average, agricultural wages compared very unfavourably with the wages obtainable in industry, despite the efforts by Joseph Arch and the National Agricultural Labourers' Union,[62] and thousands left to work in factories and on the railways or docks, where even if conditions were still hard, the hours of work were more regular and the wages greater.

As in 1851, the areas of Hall Lane, Walmer Bridge and New Longton offered more opportunities, and there were 157 employed in agriculture in these areas, compared with 115 in the immediate vicinity of Longton. Although the number of farmers cultivating small plots still predominated, there was also an increase in the number of agricultural labourers and farm servants living in. Improved farming methods now made it possible to make a reasonable living from relatively small acreages. There was, however, a noticeable increase in craftsmen, industrial workers, general labourers and those employed in gardening and general domestic work, reflecting the improvement in the overall standard of living and in the demand for goods and services among the increasing numbers of middle-class inhabitants.

Skilled workers pursued a variety of crafts. The Mawdsleys' blacksmith's business was flourishing, as was James Robinson's, who was a black and white smith. John Bond (seventy-six), together with his two sons and his partner, Obadiah Snape, ran a wheelwright's business. William Marsden of Chapel Lane and Robert Cookson of Gill Lane were also wheelwrights and may have been employed by Bond and Snape.

The Suttons' tailoring business on Liverpool Road had expanded and extended to selling drapery goods as well, and such was demand that John Johnson, also a tailor, had established a shop nearby. James Hogarth and his son William were bootmakers on Marsh Lane and Hugh Harrison of Chapel Lane made clogs. Henry Hale and his cousin Henry Caddick, who had been boot- and shoemakers in 1851, were now in their seventies and had recently retired.

Thomas Riding was a bricklayer and builder and presumably worked with his brother James who was a bricklayer and joiner. James Hart (sixteen) who lived on Marsh Lane was also a bricklayer by trade, and may have worked for the Ridings, although the Hart family were later to be well known as building contractors in the village. Other young skilled men had also moved into Longton. Thomas Benson, a joiner who had been born in Preston, and Richard Hunter, also a joiner, from Wrightington, lived with his widowed mother, who kept the Walmer Bridge Inn.

Henry Walton kept a grocer's shop on Marsh Lane, and George Pritt and James Beardsworth were grocers and flour dealers. Richard

Higham, a general dealer, lived with his farmer brother at Royalty House on Royalty Lane. Henry Scarlett of Whitestake was a provision dealer and also listed in Barrett's trade directory of 1882 as a commission agent, and may have been supplying other small local grocers. John Breatherton, who lived at Moorside, was a hay, straw and potato merchant, and by 1885, in a trade directory of that year, had extended his business to include coal, seed and lime. Mention has already been made of Philip Howard, who dealt in agricultural fertilisers and lived at The Hillock, Liverpool Road. The demand for goods of all kinds and their consequent transportation saw an increase in the number of carters and carriers, like William Banks of Gill Lane, William Taylor of Hall Lane and Thomas Alty of Marsh Lane. Charles Hawkins (twenty-one), who lived on Liverpool Road, was a cart driver and may have worked for Thomas Alty.

By 1881 both the Wilkins and Pye breweries were flourishing. Richard Wilkins was now sixty-four, and his son Thomas had taken over the brewery management, and the firm had extended its business interests into Preston. Brewing provided employment for quite a number of local men. Henry Riding was a journeyman maltster, as was William Hartley whose son George worked as his labourer. Both of them had come from Nottinghamshire. Thomas Rawcliffe worked as a cellar man and Richard Thompson and Francis Hewitson were coopers, a craft requiring considerable skill. The Wilkins's had ended their connections with the local public houses and members of the family were no longer involved as licensees. Richard Harrison now kept the Golden Ball and Frederick Stansfield the Ram's Head. The Browns continued their interest in the Farmers' Arms at Whitestake. Edward Brown, who had been only three in 1851 when his grandfather ran the business, was now in charge.

The number of men 'in service' had greatly increased, reflecting the improved standard of living locally and the developing local middle class. George Brown, who boarded with the Hawkins family on Wham Lane, was a gamekeeper and must have worked on a large estate, possibly Hutton Hall, where a full-time gamekeeper would be required. Country gentry employed gamekeepers to preserve and breed pheasants and partridges for their shooting parties and to keep down the number of rabbits. A series of Game Laws made it illegal to poach wild animals and game birds, and gamekeepers were greatly resented because the rural labourers regarded the rabbit and the odd pheasant as 'the working man's Sunday dinner'.[63] There were several gardeners. Mr and Mrs Webster living on Hall Carr Lane were both in their seventies with a private income and employed Henry Webster, who may have been a relative, as their gardener. William Carr lived in at Longton New Hall and tended the garden there, as did Henry Walwork who was the gardener for Miss Sarah Moss at the Manor House.

Thomas Dand, born at Wigton, Cumbria, was a domestic servant for the two retired ladies at Chestnut House, and Thomas Tuson worked as a domestic servant and groom to Mrs Margery Wilkins on Liverpool Road. George Hawkins, a younger brother of the cart driver Charles Hawkins, was also a groom, probably employed by the Wilkins family although he did not live in. Allen Harris, born in Hereford, worked as a coachman and lodged with William Phillipson who was a cowman, and later the Wilkins' family bailiff.

In 1881 there was still neither a doctor nor solicitor practising in the village. John Nightingale was now headmaster of Longton Free School and lived at the cottage down Marsh Lane, occupied by his predecessor Robert Wilding in 1851. Mrs Ruth Nightingale taught sewing at the school, and the eldest daughter Florence was an assistant mistress, while the younger children were cared for by their grandmother Mrs Farnworth. The Nightingales had moved around the country before settling in Longton. John Nightingale had been born at Deane, near Bolton, and his wife at Trowell in Nottinghamshire. Florence was born at King's Norton, Worcestershire, and then the family had moved to Newmarket where a further six children were born, before they left for Skelmersdale and must have come to Longton around 1880. Mr and Mrs Nightingale were very imaginative when naming their children. Florence was obviously named after Florence Nightingale, the heroine of Scutari, for the Crimean War had ended three years before she was born. The eldest son, Albert, was probably named after the Prince Consort and one of the youngest daughters was Octavia, possibly after Octavia Hill, the social reformer who pioneered the cause of the poor in the London slums and founded the National Trust.

William Marsden was Longton's police constable in 1881. Married to a local girl, he seems to have lived in the village all his married life. He no longer lived at the police station behind the Mansion House, where his predecessor Robert Whalley had lived in 1851, but in a house somewhere between West View and The Drive. A later property near the smithy on Liverpool Road was subsequently purchased by the Lancashire Constabulary in 1922 and used as a police station, but that too was sold in 2000.

Timothy Douglas, who boarded with the Harrison family on Marsh Lane, was an Excise Officer employed by the Inland Revenue. He was a bachelor originating from Callan in Ireland, but must have left to take up another post, for in Barrett's directory of 1882, a James Roche is shown as Inland Revenue Officer. Before the construction of Preston Dock in 1892, goods could still be unloaded onto Longton Marsh, and it may be that such goods had to be checked and, where necessary, excise duty levied.

By 1881, opportunities for factory work had at last come to the area – 'at Walmer Bridge an extensive cotton mill', owned by Crewdson and Grierson, was employing forty-five men and 102 women who lived in Longton and worked there as weavers. Among those who had been able to obtain work there were Thomas Wignall (seventy-two), Mark Smith (seventy) and Hugh Fiddler (fifty-six), who had been handloom weavers in 1851.

The work on the Longton section of the Preston–Southport railway line provided temporary work for quite a number of itinerant 'navvies', but also for local men. In the 1881 census there were eighteen railway labourers and eight stonemasons listed – the latter were employed to construct the bridge which spanned Liverpool Road to the south of the station. Some of the stones were removed and resited as a boundary wall to the Bentley Park housing development. Railway navvies had a reputation as tough, intemperate and belligerent men who moved from one railway construction site to the next.[64] The term 'navvy' was first used to describe the body of trained excavators or 'navigators' who travelled the country during the canal construction boom of 1791–96.

Most railway companies, particularly when constructing local lines, recruited their labour locally, and thus provided welcome work, especially for agricultural labourers when work might be difficult to find; and this was particularly so in the south of England where the higher rates of pay were attractive. Nine of the eighteen railway labourers in 1881 lived locally and the rest were lodging temporarily in the village. For poorer people who had a spare bedroom, railway labourers were an extra source of income. Two of them, Walter and Arthur Kay, born in East Lancashire, boarded with the Singleton family on Chapel Lane. The rest were all Irish from County Mayo, Sligo and County Meath. Three of them lodged with John and Mary McMahon on Hall Carr Lane. It is probable that on arriving in the village to start work, they enquired around for somewhere to stay and the McMahons were suggested, partly because they had originated from Ireland, but also because they were in their sixties and the extra income would have been welcome. Railway labouring was hard, back-breaking work, and for the raw recruit, even if he was used to agricultural work, the transition was often painful. The eighteen labourers employed in 1881 varied considerably in age and experience. Most of the Irishmen were in their thirties and forties and used to the work, but for the local men – two of them were sixteen-year-olds and Roger Higham of Gill Lane aged seventy-three – the work must have been exceedingly hard. All the stonemasons were 'boarders' and as skilled men, were used to moving from place to place as the work progressed. Three of them were born in Rufford, Scarisbrick and Bretherton and they all lodged at the Longton Arms. The others came from as far afield as Scotland, Ireland and Adlington, and their ages ranged from nineteen to fifty-five.

In terms of female occupations, there were 467 women of fifteen and over, of whom 200 worked for their living, and this was much the same ratio as in 1851. The remainder were housewives, retired or of independent means. The end of handloom weaving had had a dramatic effect on women's employment since they could no longer work at home and had to go out to work. This was a sudden and permanent break with the old domestic dual economy, and meant that those who did work were either single, widowed or older married women whose children were old enough to look after themselves while their mother was away from home. For the younger married mother work outside the home was now much more difficult, unless she had someone to care for her children. However, for many young single girls this change in the work pattern brought them much more independence and more opportunities for social contacts than were available to girls in 1851. For good or ill, women's role in society had begun to change.

The skills needed for handloom weaving were also those required for textile work in the factories. So the transfer to a factory environment, especially for the single girl, was relatively easy, and in many ways attractive, away from possible restrictions at home. In 1881 there were a hundred women working in textiles – half the local female labour force – seventy-nine were weavers, twenty winders and one warper. Over three quarters of these were single women, although 58% of them were in their teens. The rest were married, mainly young, except Eve Wignall of Chapel Lane who was sixty-seven. Many must have done as Elizabeth Hough (twenty-five) of New Longton did. She had three children under the age of five, but left them with her mother who lived next door while she worked as a weaver, and her husband as a railway labourer. Sophia Sumner (thirty-four) and widowed, had a similar arrangement. She lived on Gill Lane, but as her in-laws lived nearby on Cottam Lane she was able to leave her three-year-old twins with her sister-in-law Elizabeth Sumner. Although I have looked mainly at working women aged fifteen and over, there were two young girls, Ellen and Jane Riding, aged ten and eleven, who were employed as weavers. Crewdson and Grierson's mill at Walmer Bridge attracted very many of its employees from the families living in the vicinity, although quite a number came from Longton itself. John Clitheroe, living at Hall Green and employed as a gas maker at the gas works near the mill, had five of his children working as weavers. Thomas Whittle, who had a small holding on all Carr Lane had his four oldest daughters working at the mill.

Forty-three women and girls worked as domestic servants – only a small increase on the forty-one in 1851. Domestic service had its attractions, providing steady employment coupled with adequate board and lodging, but local girls may have preferred factory work to the loss of independence and the discipline which domestic service required. Only twelve of these domestic servants were local girls, and five came from as far away as Brighton, Chatham and Shepton Mallett. Anne Hodge (thirteen) was the niece of Edward Brown at the Farmers' Arms, where she helped her aunt Ann. Possibly her parents had a large family and felt that working with her aunt and uncle would provide her with a livelihood, and that she would gain experience while in her relatives' care. Ellen Roach (twenty-four), born in Chatham, Kent, worked as a domestic servant for the Pye brewery family on Marsh Lane, while Polly Atkins, born in Somerset, lived with her grandparents, the Jenkinses, on Gill Lane, and kept house for them. Domestic service provided for the few who might have found life difficult, like

Elizabeth Greenwood who worked for William Fowler who had a seventy-acre farm at Moorside. She was single, came from Dent in Yorkshire and had a five year-old son, Joseph, who was illegitimate. None of the women and girls in domestic service were, or had been, married, and their ages ranged from thirteen to seventy-eight year old Ellen Carr, who worked for Richard Mawdsley the blacksmith. Two elderly women worked for Mr McGuffog at the Mansion House, and had probably been in service all their lives. Betty Whitehead (seventy-six) who had been born in Padiham, was his housekeeper, and Mary Jackson (sixty-five), born in Adlington, was the housemaid. Those who were born in Longton had obviously found their jobs through family connections. This was apparent in the case of Ann Wilson (twenty-four) who was housekeeper to Robert Martin at his sixty-acre farm on Hall Green Lane, and whose father Thurston Wilson lived nearby. Elizabeth Higham worked as a domestic servant for Mrs Ann Riding, the grocer, and in all probability her sister-in-law Alice Higham, who lived on Chapel Lane, was instrumental in getting the job for her.

Domestic servants frequently became very much a part of the family for which they worked. Margery Breakell, who worked for the vicar, the Rev. John Johnson, must have moved with the family, for he had previously lived in Kirkby where Margery had been born. Similarly, Elizabeth Iddon, born in Tarleton, worked for the Rigbys who had a farm on Hall Green Lane, and had also originated from Tarleton.

In analysing women's occupations, a particular problem arose in the New Longton area due to the way in which the enumerator for that area compiled the census. Either he was short of time, or more likely misunderstood his instructions, which unfortunately did happen on occasions.[65] In most cases with unmarried girls living at home on the family farm, he classed them as 'farmer's daughters', without finding out what their duties really were. No doubt he had a problem because some of their time would be spent in the house, and some helping around the farm. But in some cases this seems to disguise what must have been an unfortunate liaison, resulting in an illegitimate child, while the family provided the daughter with an element of respectability.

For other women, running a farm was definitely a full-time job, and in all cases this was forced upon them when their husband died. There were ten widows, whose ages ranged from thirty-nine to seventy-eight, who ran farms of varying size with apparent success. Elizabeth Sargent (thirty-nine) farmed one of the largest farms, 111 acres on Chapel Lane, while Alice Whittle (seventy-eight), farmed ten acres off the turnpike.

For others, farm work could be rewarding and offer a degree of specialisation. Young Hanny (Hannah) Gemson (seventeen) worked for her uncle James Lyons at his farm near the Black Bull. Her home was in Egremont in Cumberland, which being a mining community offered little work for girls, and Hanny probably enjoyed her new life in Longton. Indeed, on census day her mother, Elizabeth, was also staying at the farm, and had obviously come down to visit Hanny and her brother who also worked there. Work as a dairymaid was specialised and no doubt offered her job satisfaction. In 1881 there were seven dairymaids, like Prudence Roscoe who worked in the dairy at the farm of her aunt, Ellen Bamber, on Chapel Lane, and Ann Cross, daughter-in-law of Thomas Cross (eighty-three) who farmed seventy-one acres at Longton Hall Farm. Alice Phillipson, married to William, who was later to be the Wilkins' farm bailiff at Holme Farm, may well have begun the tradition of the butter pats stamped with the letter 'W'.

In 1881 many more ladies were able to dress fashionably, but the age of the department store where clothes could be bought 'off the peg' had not yet arrived. Ladies' gown and outfitters' shops had developed in provincial towns, but many preferred to engage the services of a local dressmaker, and dresses seen in magazines could be copied and adapted to suit individual tastes. This gave an opportunity to women and girls with a flair for tailoring and dressmaking to set up in business locally, to cater for the requirements of the more well-to-do. It was a congenial career, which could be carried on at home and provided work which had an air of gentility about it, which factory work did not. Therefore, in contrast to 1851, when there were five dressmakers, or 'sempstresses' as they were called then, there were sixteen in 1881, reflecting the improved living standards of people's personal tastes. Ann Harrison (thirty-six), a widow living on Marsh Lane, found that her dressmaking skills helped provide for her two youngest children who were still at school, while her elder daughters were weavers. Dorothy Whittle (fifteen) lived with her parents on Hall Carr Lane. Her four elder sisters were weavers, but as she had an aptitude for sewing, she was a dressmaker's apprentice. Margaret and Agnes Bannister were also dressmakers on Marsh Lane, and probably employed the services of Eliza Chapman who lived next door and whose husband worked as a gardener.

Shopkeeping also provided a woman with an occupation which she could run from her home. I have already mentioned Ann Riding and her grocery shop at the top of Marsh Lane. Both she and later her daughter Margot were an essential part of life in Longton, and long remembered in the village. Some years ago, an elderly lady living in Chesterfield wrote to me recalling how she visited the shop as a small child and loved the smell of roasted coffee when Margot Riding allowed her to put the coffee beans into the old-fashioned grinder which stood in the corner of the shop. There were other grocers too; Ann Pickering, Margaret Gardener and Alice Caunce all kept shops on Liverpool Road.

Women and girls could also be found working in the local public houses. Mary Hunter, a widow, ran the Walmer Bridge Inn with the help of her two daughters, as did Peter Hacking's two daughters at the Red Lion. Ellen, Alice and Elizabeth Harrison helped their father at the Golden Ball, and must have been kept busy not only serving customers, but also providing meals and accommodation for lodgers and running the house.

Teaching as a profession for women offered far more opportunities than in 1851, when only one female teacher was recorded. By 1881 there were seven. Apart from Mrs and Miss Nightingale at Longton Free School, there was also Alice Scarborough, born in Colne, who lodged on Liverpool Road, and Hannah Mayor, daughter of the licensee at the Black Bull, who was seventeen and a 'pupil teacher'. Alice Bolton and Dorothy Bamber, who lived together in New Longton, taught at the Church School there which had opened in 1867.

The fact that even in 1881 there was no resident doctor in Longton poses the question of how people coped with illness and what part women played in caring for the sick in rural communities. In the nineteenth century people who lived and worked in the countryside were healthier than those living in the towns. Even though agricultural workers were paid on average two thirds of the average industrial wage and their living conditions were often insanitary and lacking in basic comforts, fresh air and the rural way of life were considerable compensations. But illnesses there were still rife. Pneumonia, bronchitis and tuberculosis were especially common and were dreaded by most folk. Older people were plagued by rheumatism, exacerbated by an ill-balanced diet and working outdoors in all weathers. Unlike today, there were no pain-killing tablets and in many rural areas people took opium to relieve pain. Opium, mixed with treacle and powdered sassafras and sold as 'Godfrey's Cordial', was often given to babies to keep them quiet. Mortality rates among children were also lower in rural areas then in the towns. In Lancashire infant deaths, even in 1893, were 193 in every 1000 in industrial towns. The diseases which, in town and country alike, were the main causes of deaths in very young children were diarrhoea, dysentery and enteritis caused by poor water supplies and inadequate hygiene.

Medical care was still very basic, and if a doctor had to be called then his fee had to be paid, unless the family contributed to a friendly society or sick club, in which case the appointed doctor would attend at no further charge. Most relied on self-help, charity or the Poor Law, although the latter meant a 'means test' and the accompanying stigma of being regarded as a pauper. Others looked to an older neighbour, especially during a confinement, and paid a small fee for her services. Many villages had 'lying-in' charities which provided the loan of 'baby bundles' to 'respectable' poor mothers in labour, which consisted of sheets and baby clothes which had to be returned after the confinement.

A whole range of homely herbal remedies could be bought or even grown – 'salts and senna', and 'brimstone and treacle' were regularly dispensed. Goose grease was rubbed on the chest to ease coughs and sore throats. Stewed groundsel was used for poultices, and camomile and yarrow leaves were brewed and drunk as a general tonic. Other practices smacked more of superstition than medicinal value, such as carrying a small potato or a whole nutmeg in the pocket to ward off rheumatism.

In some rural areas, the cottage hospital movement developed giving residential treatment to village people, and elsewhere parishes appointed their own district nurse paid for by local subscription.[66] After the 1834 Poor Law Amendment Act each Poor Law Union appointed a district medical officer, but the care provided was minimal because of the guardians' cheese-paring attitude to expenditure.

Smallpox, typhoid and diphtheria epidemics were greatly feared, and although from 1854 every infant was supposed to be vaccinated against smallpox, the disease still took its toll until 1871 when the rule was more rigidly enforced. By the turn of the century smallpox had been eradicated. Typhoid affected most rural areas until public

Liverpool Road. Church on the left, Church Row Chambers are now on the right.

health legislation forced local authorities to improve their water supplies and sewerage systems.

Illnesses such as measles, whooping cough, diptheria and scarlet fever were a fact of life for most Victorian children. Crowded together in small classrooms, children inevitably passed infection quickly from one to another, and it was not until patients were isolated and inoculation campaigns instituted that these diseases became rare

The population of the village continued to decline. By 1881 it was 1,440 – the enumerator's total is 1,443 but this is an error – a fall of 14.5% from 1851. Much Hoole, Howick and Hutton show a similar decline, but Penwortham had grown steadily, and Little Hoole, probably reflecting the building of Crewdson and Grierson's mill at Walmer Bridge, had more than doubled in size. The histogram shows a reduction in the number of young people under fifteen, representing 36.5% of the total, and agreeing with the national average at this time. 24% of the population was over forty, which is a good deal larger than the national figure.

Liverpool Road, village centre in the 1970s.

If those aged under ten years in 1851 (28.4%) had stayed in the village they would have been in the thirty to forty age group in 1881. The histogram shows that this age group represents only 17.5% of the 1881 population, and it is assumed that, allowing for those who had died, the majority had migrated out of the village in those thirty years.

Among the sexes, there are slightly more girls than boys in the early years, but in the older groups neither sex predominates and there is no clear reflection of the national trend for women to outlive men.

In 1881, 57% of the population had been born in Longton – a fall of 7% on the 1851 figure. Of those who had migrated into the village, although the majority (18%) still came from the villages and townships within a five mile radius, 7% came from elsewhere in the British Isles (the number of Irish navvies working on the West Lancashire Railway and only temporarily resident does inflate the figure). Of the 291 households, 44% had one or both parents who had come to the village at some stage, and this again is somewhat surprising compared with the figure of 56% in 1851, especially as one would expect that the workforce would have become increasingly mobile as the century wore on. It must therefore be assumed that, after the trauma created by the end of handloom weaving, the village settled back into an earlier migration pattern, which partained until the turn of the century, when the population once again began to increase.

The 'migrants' again consisted of craftsmen — bootmakers, wheelwrights and blacksmiths, dealers and carters, several working in the brewery trade, and also farm and general labourers. James Hogarth, a bootmaker, had been born in Garstang and had worked in Preston prior to coming to Longton. Obadiah Snape, a wheelwright, was born at Wheelton, and his partner John Bond at Withnell. William Hartley, a journeyman maltster, born in Nottinghamshire, had moved to the village about 1877. Richard Thompson, a cooper, came from Ulverston and had worked in Barrow-in-Furness. Francis Hewitson, also a cooper, had been born in Lancaster and worked in Preston before coming to Longton, and Charles Hawkins, cart driver, was born in Mountain Ash, Glamorgan; Henry Scarlet, a provision dealer, had been born in Suffolk and his wife in Accrington. Most of the farm labourers and their wives came from neighbouring villages, but John Jenkins had been born in Milford Haven and his wife in Somerset.

Husbands born in Longton and owning or tenanting farms, particularly if they came from families which had been in the village for several generations, almost inevitably seem to have married girls also born in the village. There were of course good reasons for this. Family ties and local connections were still strong, and if the girl was an only daughter, there could be an opportunity to increase the size of the joint family holding. Whether this was deliberate, thereby creating a form of local 'closed shop', we shall never know.

In 1881, 56.6% of the population was or had been married, compared with 59% in 1851. Slightly fewer in the age group twenty to thirty, 62.4%, were unmarried, and of those over thirty years of age, one in five still remained single. However, in the age group thirty to forty, slightly more women were single than in 1851, but fewer men remained bachelors. This indicates that improved job opportunities for men made them more optimistic about settling down to married life, whereas increased work outside the home may have encouraged women to have a rather more independent attitude to marriage.

Many of those in the older groups who remained single were from local farming families, and had the same pressures as in 1851 of finding land for themselves, or staying at home with an elderly parent.

The over-sixties represented 10% of the total population in 1881 compared with 7.8% in 1851, reflecting the fact that people were living longer, due to improved diet and general living standards. This inevitably produced an increase in the numbers of widows and widowers – ninety-one in 1881 and fifty-eight in 1851. About a third lived with married sons or daughters as part of an extended family, and again, where land was involved, were still classed as 'head of the household'.

As in 1851, widows often lived close to their married children, and which meant there was mutual help and support. Margaret Carr (sixty-nine) and her sister Ellen Sumner (seventy-one) lived on Gill Lane next door to Ellen's widowed daughter-in-law, Sophia. Classed as 'nurses' on the census, they probably cared for Sophia's three children while she worked as a weaver. Several widows and widowers lived alone and were able to afford to employ servants who lived in. William Fowler (fifty-seven) farmed seventy acres at Moorside. Born at Alston in Cumberland, he employed Dixon Crumsly, also from Alston, and James Bentham and Elizabeth Greenwood from Dent, as farm and domestic servants.

There were 131 family units in 1881, of which 103 were nuclear, and the remainder extended families. Most couples had only one or two children, compared with the average of four in 1851. However, the gap between one child and the next was less, being two years, rather than the three of thirty years before. There seems no significance or connection between the size of the family and the occupation of the father. Although it appears that most parents were deliberately limiting the size of their families, there were still examples of large ones.

William and Ann Taylor of Hall Lane had nine children ranging from Elizabeth (twenty-two) to Annie (four months). John Johnson the tailor, and his wife Jane of Liverpool Road, also had a family of nine from Jane (twenty) to Robert (twelve months). Because the average family unit was smaller, fewer women were still having children in their forties, but again there were exceptions. Ann Parker (forty-seven) a farmer's wife of Hall Carr Lane had a ten-month-old daughter, her eighth child, and Elizabeth Higham (sixty) of Wham Lane had a daughter aged twelve. But some women had their first child when they were still in their teens. Betsy Hacking (forty-one), the licensee's wife at the Red Lion, had a daughter aged twenty-four and Alice Harrison (thirty-two) of Marsh Lane had a daughter, Ellen, aged seventeen and subsequently five other children.

Unmarried brothers and sisters continued to live together as they had done in 1851. James and John Walton ran their small farm on Chapel Lane, while their sisters Dorothy and Ann worked as cotton weavers, and a third sister, Maria, was a dairymaid and also seems to have kept house for them all. Living with them were Joseph and Harriet, a nephew and niece, and this was a fairly common arrangement where older children were boarded out with members of the same family.

Family members also continued to live in close proximity to one another, providing mutual help. Henry Knowles farmed fifty-seven acres on Chapel Lane and had a family of seven children. Next door lived Betty Knowles (seventy), his mother, together with his unmarried brother William and sister Margaret. Richard Hough (sixty-six) and his wife and two unmarried children lived next door to Benjamin Hough (twenty-six), a railway labourer, and his young family, while William Hough (thirty-one) and his family lived nearby on Wham Lane. The Nelsons, also at New Longton, seemed to have been a particularly close-knit family. James Nelson (twenty-three) and his wife and small son lived together with his widowed uncle William and his grandfather James (seventy-nine). John Nelson, a younger brother, and his family lived close by at Royalty Cottages, and next door to them, another uncle and his family.

Families continued to give mutual support when problems arose. Roger Higham (seventy-three) lived on Gill Lane with two single daughters and two unmarried sons, together with a 'daughter' aged eleven months, who must have been the child of either Dorothy (twenty-two) or Elizabeth (twenty). Similarly, Thomas Bamber (seventy-two) of Chapel Lane had a 'son' aged one who must have been the illegitimate child of one of his spinster daughters. So by 1881, although there were a few cases of illegitimacy, there was still an element of stigma attached to it, and a consequent reluctance to reveal this to the census enumerator.

Physical disability associated with old age was a general problem, which Edward and Amelia Holt solved by having Edward's blind and widowed father Henry (seventy-nine) to live with them on Hall Lane. Richard Hosker, who farmed twenty-nine acres on Moss Hall Lane, had his widowed mother Ellen (seventy-eight), who was also blind, living with him, while his younger brother, Henry, lived with his family next door.

CHAPTER NINE

Church, Chapel and School

THE VICTORIAN AGE was a period, unlike today, of religious observance. Religion dominated the lifestyle of the middle class. It was respectable to attend church or chapel every Sunday. Victorian homes were filled with framed homilies and Biblical texts such as 'God is Love' and 'The Lord is my Shepherd', and in some at least, regular prayers and Bible readings were obligatory. Outward religious observance and 'good' works suited the moral and ethical code of the Victorian middle class and differentiated them from the lower orders. Christianity permeated national life and its legal framework. Blasphemy was an indictable offence and the Lord's Day Observance Society banned games and entertainments and even sober activities such as visiting museums, which were closed on Sundays even in London until 1900.[67] To the world at large, England was a Christian country, exemplifying the Christian ethics and beliefs which

Opposite: The Interior of St Andrew's Church, Longton.

were essential to living a moral life. This created dismay among foreigners who found it difficult to come terms with the 'English Sunday'.

Yet how deep these convictions were must remain the personal view of the historian. Certainly for many, religion was a mark of their respectability and status in society, and any deviation from it spelt social and professional ruin. The increase in prostitution was evidence that many men adopted double standards, and although outwardly pillars of society and respected family providers, their 'leisure' activities were often very different, while their wives and children lived in pious but claustrophobic domesticity.[68] Servants were allowed time off to attend church or chapel, but were worked from morning to night for the rest of the week. Middle class families read *Oliver Twist* or Kingsley's *Water Babies* but turned a blind eye to the plight of the workhouse child or the chimney sweep. Therefore, although many did put their religious principles into practical efforts to help the poor and under-privileged, many more, who preached respectability and moral rectitude, were hypocrites.

For women, however, the church and chapel gave them their own social life outside the home, organising church bazaars, chapel teas outings and helping with the Sunday school. In addition, there was a host of charities, locally and nationally, which needed fundraisers and local voluntary helpers. These ranged from neighbourly care for the poor and elderly, caring for the bereaved and running local

St Andrew's Church, Longton.

dispensaries, to national organisations for unmarried mothers and 'fallen women', ragged schools and missionary societies. In this way well-to-do women were able get away from the often stultifying atmosphere of their homes, and in many cases to assuage their feelings of guilt through good works. The recipients of these charitable efforts were probably grateful, but whether they also resented being patronised we shall never know. Many people were therefore surprised and in some cases shocked by the findings of the religious census which was taken of all those attending a place of public worship on 30 March, 1851. Out of the 18 million people living in England and Wales, nearly 7 million had been to church or chapel on that day. Allowing for inaccuracies and the fact that some people were counted twice on that Sunday, the figures revealed that over 40% of the population did attend a place of public worship. More people in country areas and in the smaller towns went to a religious service than did those living in the large industrial towns. The working classes largely regarded the Anglican clergy as remote, both in their social and political life. The gulf between the wealthy vicar with his comfortable stipend and his additional income from his tithes, and the poor curate, created nothing but unpopularity, and even contempt.

By the 1830s some Anglican clergy had become aware of this, and by the 1850s the Church realised that it had to adopt a populist evangelical approach if it was to be effective, especially in the new industrial areas. Churches were repaired, new ones built, church schools were established and there was a drive to involve the laity in social activities in the parishes.

Yet for many, even this greater community-oriented approach by the Anglican hierarchy was not what they were seeking from religion. Methodism, even though within its compass there were divisions between Wesleyans, the Primitive Methodists and the New Connexion, provided the answer for some.

For others, the Baptists, Unitarians and Quakers appealed. Roman Catholicism, with its principal support in the north of England, was especially strong in Lancashire, and in towns like Preston, Liverpool and Wigan, its adherents outnumbered those of other congregations. With the influx of Irish labourers in the 1850s it too had to rethink its role, and encompass the new predominantly working class. The Mormon missionaries who arrived in Liverpool in 1837 and preached in and around Preston offered a radical religion, coupled with a new challenge in the New World. Between 1850 and 1870 some 22,000 left the north-west to make the trek across the prairies and mountains to Salt Lake City, Utah.

Yet the churches of all denominations did much to improve the lot of the ordinary people. They established day and Sunday schools, even though the working-class child was still taught to 'know his place' and not have 'ideas above his station'. Most children accepted the religious indoctrination quite happily and remembered the familiar hymns and Bible stories with nostalgia, even if the depth of their subsequent religious commitment varied. For others their memories were largely of outings by wagonette followed by tea on the vicarage lawn. Some clergy especially were remembered their genuine concern in providing clothes for the

St Andrew's Church. The east window (left) depicts the Crucifixion. The Wilkins' Window in the South aisle (right) is in memory of Thomas and Fanny Wilkins who died in 1927.

poorest children, medicine and special foods during illness and extra tuition for the bright child. Many adults took an active part as Sunday School teachers, while non-conformist chapels, especially in the cities, ran Bible classes for young men and women and like the Anglican church organised help for the poor and sick, and formed missionary societies.

Gradually, however, the influence of both church and chapel dwindled. The counter-attraction to the country labourer of a day of rest from hard physical work was too strong, and the town worker had the choice of the pub, the theatre or the music hall. Among the more committed, the conflict between science and religion deepened after the publication of Darwin's *On the Origin of Species by Means of Natural Selection* in 1859. Were the Old Testament stories about the creation of the world purely legends, and if natural laws were scientific fact, how could the miracles be explained? Intellectuals found the churches increasingly irrelevant, but many church-goers reached some form of personal compromise, based on the moral and ethical message of Christianity.

Religion did, however, foster the link in the establishment of wider educational provision. Before the 1870s, education was largely provided by a variety of voluntary and private enterprise. This encompassed the public schools, such as Eton, Harrow and Rugby, and the local grammar schools, many of which were sixteenth-century foundations, and catered for the sons of the nobility and gentry and well-to-do tradesmen; and the Sunday schools, ragged schools and dame schools and classes organised by the vicar for local children. No qualifications were required and therefore schools varied enormously in the quality of teaching provided; nor was school attendance obligatory. In 1851, of the 5 million school-age children, 600,000 were working, just over 2 million were at school, and the rest were neither at school or at work. There was undoubtedly a desire by many working-class parents that their children should be educated, but this depended on several factors. A steady income was necessary to provide the weekly school contribution, and inevitably skilled artisans and the better-paid workers in a secure job were conscious of the benefits of education for their children. But local influences from family, the church and chapel were also important, and here the Sunday School movement had a considerable effect on fostering basic literacy values.

The approved day schools, largely financed by

the National Society which was Church of England, the British and Foreign Schools Society which was Non-Conformist, and other religious bodies, provided premises and equipment, paid the teachers' salaries and controlled what should be taught. State aid was given to such organisations based on a system of 'payment by results'. By 1862, Government became anxious to to ensure that its grant aid was used efficiently, and appointed school inspectors who annually tested each child in the three Rs and checked school attendance records. This system, which persisted until 1890, assessed progress in a series of standards from one to six, and failure resulted in the withdrawal of grant from the school. It was an unpopular system. Teachers as well as pupils developed a feeling of hysteria and dread as the day of the inspection drew near. The rules, which allowed those pupils who had put in the required number of attendances to go to work for the rest of the year, did not help teachers to present a true picture of their school on examination day. Inspectors also disliked giving a poor report which might result in the loss of grant. Eventually, in 1897 the system was changed and inspections could be made without prior notice and thus a more accurate assessment of normal school work could be made.[69]

The voluntary system did not cover all parts of the country, and the Education Act of 1870 established that local School Boards should be set up to provide elementary schools financed from local rates and to enforce the attendance of all children over the age of five living in the area. School attendance was a source of considerable conflict between the authorities and parents, especially in country areas where traditionally children had always helped with the harvest or with jobs around the farm. In the 1850s it was not unusual for children as young as six to work at simple jobs such as stone-picking, bird-scaring and minding the sheep and pigs. In the early autumn, large numbers helped with the corn and hay harvest and potato and turnip picking.[70]

In 1851 in Longton, the census reveals that many young children did not attend school, but were either earning by handloom weaving or helping with jobs around the home. Thomas and Alice Parker on Marsh Lane had four children – the eldest boys aged one and twelve were weavers, and the two girls aged eight and nine were certainly not at school. Similarly, James Hoskinson on Marsh Lane had three children aged between nineteen and five who were not at school. Other parents sent their children to school when they were at a young age, but then withdrew them as they got older, feeling they were better employed in contributing to the family income. John Hartley, a farm labourer at Walmer Bridge, had two elder daughters, Ellin (eleven) and Margaret (nine), working as handloom weavers, while his two youngest, William (seven) and Alice (four), went to school.

Legislation enacted between 1875 and 1891 to reduce the use of child labour on the land was totally ineffective, primarily because of the many exemptions and loop holes which the laws allowed, but also because the fees of a penny or two pence a week per child were a problem for parents when the father was unemployed or there was a large family. Equipping children for school was also very often a real struggle for poor parents. Boots, which were worn by both boys and girls, were expensive. Boys often had to wear their fathers' cut-down trousers and mothers were adept at 'make do and mend', but despite their best efforts, some children suffered bullying and ridicule from better-off pupils. Not until 1891, when school fees were abolished for elementary education, and increased agricultural mechanisation and the conversion from arable to pastoral farming made child labour less necessary, was compulsory school attendance achievable.

The Victorian school was very different from most schools today. Not all were purpose-built, and especially in the country areas were held in cottages or the local vicarage or chapel. The school-room, heated by an open fire, was often cold in winter except for those

sitting nearest to it, and airless in summer. Children sat at their desks in rows, and lessons were basically the three Rs, religious instruction and singing, with sewing for the girls. Slates were used for learning to write and then pupils progressed to copy books. Reading books, written specifically for children, were boring and frequently overlaid with sickly moral sentimentality. After the 1860s, history, geography, grammar and drawing were added to the curriculum, but this was often no more than learning a string of dates and facts. Physical education and drill became a regular activity each week. Discipline was often harsh, and enforced by the use of the cane, but most children accepted this, being used to correction at home. Some teachers were barely literate, and where there were large classes, use was made of the 'monitor' system where older pupils supplemented the work of teachers. Later, the pupil-teacher scheme, established by James Kay-Shuttleworth, enabled older, bright scholars to be apprenticed to a teacher to help with class teaching and later to complete their training with a period of full-time study. By the turn of the century, although classes were still large by today's standards, teachers were better trained and some School Boards provided secondary education, and thereby the opportunity for bright working class children to obtain further qualifications, but there was insufficient provision of scholarships to enable many to achieve this. Even so, most children left school at the age of ten, subsequently raised to eleven in 1893, and to thirteen in 1914.

In spite of the rigid emphasis on discipline, the learning by rote, the inadequacy of school buildings and the lack of appreciation of the emotional and physical development of the child, nineteenth-century education did, for the first time, provide basic literacy and numeracy for the large majority of children and many

Opposite page: Village school, on the right in the top view, Liverpool Road. Now demolished.

looked back on their school days with some affection, often associated with the efforts of a kind and able teacher.[71]

The development of religion and education in nineteenth-century Longton was bedevilled by its past, and in order to explain how the church and the schools developed, it is necessary to go back many centuries.

In its religious life, the village had early links with the church of St Mary's Penwortham, and these remained until as late as 1938 when Longton eventually became a separate parish. In 1140 the Abbey of Evesham, which owned land in this locality, was required to provide a priory and three priests to say services at Penwortham, and this was confirmed in 1150 by a later document which was witnessed by 'Eafward, the priest of Longton'. This implies that if there was a priest at Longton in 1150, it was likely there was a church of some sort also.

Late-fourteenth-century documents refer to 'clericus de Longton', probably a lay brother or clerk in minor orders, but it appears that the priory at Penwortham made little impact on the surrounding locality, being remote from the mother house at Evesham, and in an area which was impassable 'at divers seasons of the year by the abundance of water', and its duty to 'keep schools in the villages and teach small boys without a fee' seems to have been ignored.

In 1517, however, William Walton, 'chaplain of Longton' and connected to a well-to-do family from Ulnes Walton and Hoole, provided land for the endowment of a chantry chapel in the village. He also provided for a priest to say services at the chapel and to 'teach and instruct the poor children of the inhabitants there grammar, if he could conveniently do so'. Unfortunately, and although well-intentioned, William Walton could not foresee the effects which the Reformation and Henry VIII's dissolution of the Church lands might have on his endowment, and many hundreds like it. By means which are no longer clear, his nephew Christopher Walton

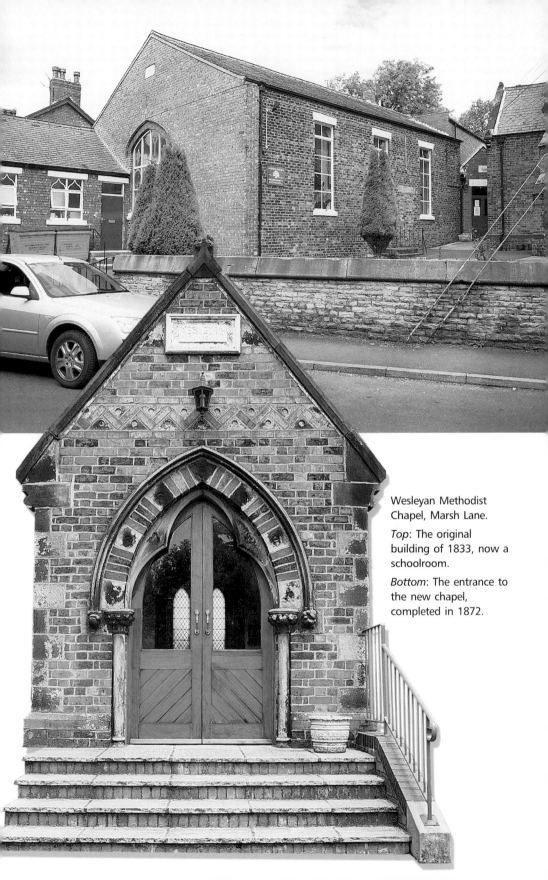

Wesleyan Methodist Chapel, Marsh Lane.

Top: The original building of 1833, now a schoolroom.

Bottom: The entrance to the new chapel, completed in 1872.

took over the endowment and cleverly argued that the original endowment was primarily for educational purposes, thus saving it from sequestration. In 1552 he founded a school at 'a convenient place to serve the parish of Penwortham', and although there was no reference to his uncle's earlier endowment, Longton chapel was chosen as the place for the new school. This ingenious scheme enabled the the school to be maintained from the funds originally intended for the chantry chapel. The only problem, however, was that this ostensibly left no money to pay the resident priest at the chapel. As a result, until 1751, the chapel was served by a succession of schoolmasters, some of whom were ordained priests who took the regular services and attended as far as possible to the pastoral needs of the parish. The congregation was not happy about this situation, and by 1720 had petitioned the Bishop of Chester: 'it is the humble request of the inhabitants that the chapel be supplied by a regular licensed priest.' The old chantry chapel, now some 250 years old, was in a sorry state, and in 1766 it is recorded that 'The Chapel of Longton is . . . a very ancient structure but through length of time is become so ruinous and in decay and in so great danger of falling that the Parishioners are afraid, foundation, Walls and Roof being very greatly decayed'. Meanwhile a grant from Queen Anne's Bounty in 1791, and the donation of land from the lords of the manor, made it possible at long last to pay a resident curate and to plan for the building of a new church. In 1772 the old building was demolished and a new chapel built on the same site in the following year. It was a simple structure, with plastered exterior walls, a porch at the west end and above it a gallery for the choir. Between 1773 and 1887 this chapel catered for the spiritual needs of the parish, but as elsewhere, the spread of non-conformity made its impact on Longton.

In 1807 a Wesleyan chapel was built on Marsh Lane, and replaced by a more permanent structure in 1833. With the increase in its congregation, another chapel, with red brick exterior and a blue slate roof, was built in 1872 and the older building converted into a Sunday schoolroom. The Primitive Methodists had built their own chapel on Chapel Lane in 1837, but the congregation dwindled and the building was eventually converted into two houses, now numbered 57 and 59 Chapel Lane. A licence to build a Congregational meeting house was granted in 1821 but this was never built.

The Mormon mission had a considerable impact on the religious life of the village – 'during the crusade, both the Protestant church and the Wesleyan chapel of the village were for a time rather seriously shattered'. The Wesleyan place of worship was nearly emptied. Indeed two Mormon missionaries, Orson Hyde and Heber Kimball, came to Longton on 26 December 1837 and preached their message to those assembled on Longton Marsh. Ten were baptised that day and more on the day following, despite the severe cold weather – 'in the cold brine of the open sea, when the temperature was such that fresh water streams were frozen thick with ice'.[72] It is alleged that £100 was contributed locally towards the cost of the sect's first printing press and undoubtedly some Longton folk must have been among those converts who later set sail from Liverpool for the New World.

It was not until 1894 that the Roman Catholic community in the village got its own place of worship, when St Oswald's mission chapel was opened, consisting of a church, school and presbytery. In 1925, it became the mother church for a new larger parish and by 1965, with the increased number of parishioners, a new church was built and officially opened.

By 1870, the Anglican chapel congregation, in common with others all over the country, wanted to replace the old building with a new church, for although still part of the St Mary's Penwortham, Longton regarded itself as a separate parish in all but name. A building fund was established, but raising sufficient capital took time. The fund was a parish memorial to the

Rev. Charles Astbury, the previous incumbent who had died in 1873, and initially raised some £400 together with a personal gift of £630. A subsequent bazaar in the Preston Corn Exchange in September 1878 raised a further £950, and the building, designed by J. and J. Cutts of London, was begun in 1886 and finally consecrated by the Bishop of Manchester in December, 1887. Meanwhile a report of 1901[73] refers to a school which had been erected in 1867, and in 1878 premises to house a school-master or mistress were also erected.

The grammar school established by Christopher Walton in 1552 provided a classical elementary education on payment of 'cock-pence' twice yearly to all children living within the Penwortham township. ('Cockpence' may have been similar to capon rents paid by medieval tenants to the lord of the manor.) In the early years it was held in Longton chapel, but during the 1620s was transferred to a cottage nearby, on what is now School Lane.[74] Careful management of the trust's estate enabled a new building to be erected in 1746–7 at Hutton, which, with radical alterations and additions, is the Hutton Grammar School of today. With the building of the new school, the old practice of combining the post of schoolmaster and curate of Longton chapel finally came to an end.

In 1826, the Charity Commission had reported[75] that elemen-tary schools had also been established by public subscription in Farington and Howick and that a school at Cop Lane, Penwor-tham, was planned. These schools also formed part of the Grammar School foundation and received support from its funds. Christopher Walton's endowment had provided for the original school, but also brought with it lands which his uncle William had donated to provide the chantry chapel. These 'messuages, burgages, lands, tenements and hereditaments' were scattered in 'the townships of Kirkham, Kellamergh and Preston', and had later been added to by a trust deed of 1606 to include land in Longton and Hutton as well. After Christopher's death, the administration of the school and lands was entrusted to several of the landed gentry in the locality, and subsequently to their heirs and successors. By using the rents from these estates, the trustees were able to maintain the grammar school and assist financially with the later elementary schools which I have mentioned. Administering the trust must have been time-consuming and complicated and it appears that in 1826 the Charity Commission found considerable cause for criticism in the work of the trustees. Properties in Preston, for example, had been leased at an agricultural rent taking no account of the fact that the property in the centre of Preston could command a much higher rent due to pressure on land for building purposes at the time. It was obvious that the trustees needed not only professional and legal advice in managing the endowment's finances, but needed to exert more effective control over the quality of education provided.

However, little seemed to have been done to improve matters. In 1865, Mr Bryce, acting for the Schools Inquiry Commissioners, made an inspection and found much to criticise. The work was of an 'elementary character' and there was a 'highly paid staff in comparison with the work done', while the number of pupils had fallen by half since the earlier inspection of 1826. Subsequently in 1876, after a public meeting in Penwortham, the Commission and the trustees agreed a scheme to put the whole foundation onto a more effective and professional footing.

The curriculum should consist of reading, writing and arithmetic, geography and history, English grammar, composition and literature, Latin, a foreign language, a natural science, drawing, vocal music and drill and religious instruction according to the doctrine of the Church of England. Admission was to be by entrance examination: foundation scholarships were to be offered and boarders would be accommodated. By 1899, when a further inspection took place, much had been achieved.

New schools had been built at Howick, Cop Lane and Farington, and provided elementary education with an Anglican bias. The trustees also resolved the thorny problem of Longton Free School, which had caused difficulties ever since its endowment in 1793. As in the case of William Walton's endowment of 1517, the good intentions of the benefactor were superseded by later events. After the new grammar school built at Hutton in 1746–7, there was no school in Longton. In 1793, Robert Moss had left money to build a school for the education of children of the township, and by 1806, the bequest had accumulated sufficiently for a school to be built on Marsh Lane. Children were taught 'reading, writing and accounts' for an annual payment of a shilling for 'firing' to heat the building. Unfortunately, the endowment never had sufficient capital either to maintain the school or pay the schoolmaster adequately, and in 1821 it was closed. The pupils were transferred to the church in the centre of the village. The dual use of the building as a day school on weekdays and a Sunday school created interminable problems of responsibility between the chapel and the foundation, but by 1899 these were resolved. Subsequently this school too became obsolete when the new county primary school was built on School Lane in 1926. By 1900, therefore, Longton had places of worship and Sunday schools for the main religious denominations. It had its Free School and opportunities for more academic pupils at Hutton Grammar School, and there were elementary schools on the outskirts at Howick, New Longton,and Hoole, where a church school had been built in 1850.

Just how many parents sent their children to school can be seen from census returns. In 1851 there were 318 children in the age group four to ten years (145 boys and 173 girls), of whom 60% were classed as 'scholars'. There were fifty children over the age of ten who attended school. Those parents who kept their children at home came from various occupations – weavers, farmers, labourers and carters, and a fair number lived in New Longton,

Old School, Marsh House Lane, latterly Bob Gamble's barber's shop, now demolished. Robert Moss endowed this building, its date stamp read, 'Founded by R.M. Moss 1803'. Renovated and refurbished into the present building.

where, of course, there was no school until 1867. Nevertheless I found references to the establishment of a night school at New Longton opened in 1867 and, together with the day school, was under the auspices of the Anglican church and presumably offered basic education in the three Rs to young people who were working during the day. By the census of 1881, and following the Act of 1870, a much larger proportion of local children attended school. In the age group four to ten years, there were 242 children (120 boys and 122 girls), of whom 88% were classed as 'scholars'. The absentees were primarily farmers' children. Of those over ten years, 66% (thirty-seven boys and twenty-nine girls) were still attending school.

Although religion came to mean less and less to very many people in Lancashire in the nineteenth century, for many rural folk, the church and chapel still offered a focal point for much of their social life. This was certainly true for women and children

and is apparent from what we know of Longton during this time. Children who attended church schools were expected to attend Sunday school as well. This was welcomed by many parents, who at least on Sunday afternoons could have some time to themselves away from the children. Sunday school largely consisted of Bible readings and learning the catechism, and was usually run by the vicar with volunteer helpers.[76]

It is significant, however, that by 1914, of the 6 million who attended Sunday schools, few became committed church-goers as adults. Nevertheless, these Sunday gatherings maintained a bond of 'belonging' at a time when the old bonds of rural society were beginning to break down. Most enjoyed the classes, and by blending class work with social events, teachers could maintain the interest not only of the younger children, but teenagers as well. In rural areas, Whitsun Walks, magic lantern shows and annual outings were major events, not only for the scholars but for their parents too. Day schools often had their annual concerts and of course there was Harvest Festival and carol-singing in church and chapel at Christmas time.

The connection between the church and the local gentry still remained, even after the Tithe Commutation Act of 1836, for the Rawstorne family of Penwortham Priory retained the patronage of the living of St Andrew's, Longton. Socially this provided local people with the occasional opportunity of mixing with the gentry. In 1863, at his coming of age, Lawrence Rawstorne held a dinner in celebration at which 250 major tenants and other local gentry were entertained. In the afternoon 400 sat down to a tea of 'beef pies, veal pies, sandwiches and Ribble salmon', followed by dancing. There was also tea for young people at Penwortham Sunday school. Unfortunately, heavy rain after lunch

Opposite page: St Oswald's R.C. Church and presbytery. The war memorial was provided by an anonymous donor.

saw many best bonnets ruined and floral decorations and flags at Howick were also damaged.

National events like Queen Victoria's Diamond Jubilee in June 1897 were also celebrated locally by Longton's church and chapel.

A pole forty-seven feet long had been planted by the wardens on the side of the tower to reach sixteen feet above the ridge of the roof of the church, and a red sign was seen floating on it from the 19th for ten days. White ensigns were flying on the school and the parsonage. The interior of the church was decorated with the Royal Standard, a large blue ensign, several small Union Jacks and the Sunday School banner:

> The church and chapel Sunday schools joined together to make their annual 'treats' a Jubilee fete, and a procession through the village was led by the Freckleton brass band. They had a good tea at the church school and afterwards formed a second procession to The Grove grounds where Mr Wilkins kindly threw open his gardens for them. He floated a large Union Jack on a lofty pole and had erected a large tent in which he gave light provisions. An attempt was made to send off balloons but owing to a wind springing up two of them caught fire early and a third, after rising to a considerable height also took fire. Everything passed off quite orderly and they enjoyed a happy day.

CHAPTER TEN

Agriculture and the Coming of the Railway

*P*RIOR to the eighteenth century, farming in Longton had hardly changed. Enclosure of small areas of land had taken place alongside the cultivation of strips in the open fields from an early period. Indeed Lancashire as a whole had never suffered the bitter disputes over land enclosure which occurred elsewhere in England. Individual strips were consolidated either by exchange or purchase, and waste and marshy land was enclosed from a very early date. The reclaimed land was allotted by local agreement, and by custom, tenants were allowed small parcels of this moss land from which to extract peat. These were called 'moss pieces' or 'moss rooms'. This right, known as the right of turbary, was jealously guarded, for peat was an invaluable source of fuel for heating and cooking, at a time when the cost of coal from the colliery areas was prohibitive for most local people.

But the gradual growth in the village population put increasing pressure on the available land, and an obvious answer was to make more use of the extensive mosslands on the outskirts of the village. The potential of these areas became apparent as the techniques of land drainage became more widely known. Longton Marsh had been enclosed by Act of Parliament in the 1720s. In 1760 a further

750 acres were enclosed, enabling the effective drainage of the large area of natural mossland around New Longton to take place. The tracks which gave access to this area are still preserved in names such as Moss Lane, Long Moss Lane and Wholesome Lane.

By 1851, farmsteads had been established and land brought into permanent cultivation on this reclaimed land. But despite this, much remained to be done to improve the condition of the soil, especially in the areas nearest to the village. For centuries the land had been regularly fertilised by marling, and evidence of these old marl pits can still be seen on present-day maps of the Longton area. Marl deposits could be found at a depth of some three to five feet below ground and were dug out and spread on the fields to reduce their acidity. But Lawrence Rawstorne, writing on farming in the area in 1843, drew attention to the backwardness of the methods used, primarily because handloom weaving had taken precedence over any other activity. Farms had been subdivided and cottages built, with space for handlooms added, all in the interests of making money out of weaving. But with the demise of weaving, tenants could only eke out a basic existence and had nothing left over for land improvements. Rawstorne stressed the need to diversify the types of crops grown and to plant turnips, potatoes, carrots and nitrogenous plants such as clover and vetches, and although this had already begun in a small way, more determined effort was required. He was not alone in urging improvements in agricultural methods, particularly in soil improvement to meet the demands of the industrial towns for agricultural produce. In 1839, the Royal Agricultural Society had led an investigation into the properties of various types of manure.[77] The amount of waste material produced by the new towns from night-soil, from privies and from market refuse and street-sweeping was enormous, and could with sufficient enterprise have provided ample manure for their surrounding rural areas. The problems lay not only in its collection, but also in its storage, for manure was only required occasionally and furthermore it needed to be diluted before use. Because there were no adequate sewerage systems at this time, the efficient use of urban waste remained unsolved, despite the evidence that the accumulation of such waste seriously contributed to the danger of epidemics. Some experiments in the production of liquid manure were made by constructing reservoirs for urine, which could be added to compost from stables and cowsheds, but these were exceptions. Many farmers could not afford the initial outlay and others were conservative in attitude. Eventually a cheap and easier substitute in the form of guano – sea bird droppings first imported into Liverpool in 1835 – became available. Easy to store, less odorous than dung and very effective as a fertiliser, it is not surprising that in 1881, Longton farmers were using it, supplied by Philip Howard who is listed in the census for that year as a guano, bone and manure dealer.

The history of land tenure in Longton is complicated. In common with much of Lancashire, Longton was never the typical textbook manorial village, with the manor house, occupied by the lord and his family, surrounded by his tenants, farming their individual strips in the great open fields. Originally comprising two manors, over the centuries, either by marriage, inheritance or purchase, these were subdivided, until by the seventeenth century the Fleetwoods of Penwortham, the Ashtons of Croston, the Heskeths of Rufford and the Shireburnes of Stonyhurst all owned land in the parish and lordship of their respective estates. But these estates were not neat recognisable entities, for piecemeal land acquisition over the centuries had left their holdings scattered throughout the area. Significantly, because none of the four lords lived in the village, the tight control which a resident lord would have imposed was never exercised. The wealthier local tenants thus controlled their own affairs to a much greater extent than in the typical manorial village. Nevertheless, the traditional system of agriculture whereby the villagers cultivated the land on the basis of individual strips, allocated according to each tenant's status, went on in Longton just as it did all over England. Each strip was between a half and one acre and they were distributed over the great open fields so that the best and poorest land was evenly shared. Each strip was divided from its neighbour by a furrow made by the turn of the plough. The furrow drained the surface water from the ridge or 'rig' where the crops were grown. Evidence of this distinctive 'rig and furrow', made by the long hump-backed ridges with furrows between, can still be seen, for example, on the recreation ground behind the Black Bull Inn. Evidence too of strip cultivation is clearly seen in the long narrow fields which run northwards between Marsh Lane and Back Lane.

By 1838 when the Tithe Award was drawn up, it is clear that the fortunes of the principal landowners had fluctuated since the early years of the seventeenth century.

The Heskeths still retained ownership through Sir Thomas Dalrymple Hesketh Bart, but the Ashton and Fleetwood estates had passed to Thomas Joseph Trafford and Robert Moss respectively. When Mary, Duchess of Norfolk, the last of the Shireburnes, died without male issue, the estates had passed to Edward Weld, and subsequently by 1838 to Joseph Weld.

Sir Thomas D. Hesketh owned about 285 acres, with eleven farms and two smallholdings, all leased to local tenants who farmed the land and lived in the farmhouses which went with the tenancies. His principal tenant was James Cox with seventy-two acres at Thornton Barn.

Thomas Trafford owned some 320 acres, with eleven farms and a smallholding. He also owned eight cottages and three houses, one of which was Plumpton House on Marsh Lane, tenanted by Thomas Wilkins. His chief farm tenant was James Tuson with sixty-six acres off Gill Lane and still known as Tuson's Farm.

Joseph Weld's estate comprised 385 acres with seven farms and three cottages. His principal tenant was George Taylor, who lived and worked at Longton Hall Farm, which at 129 acres was the largest in the village. In 1840, however, the farm was sold to a Mr Garstang for £555, although George Taylor's widow still lived in the farmhouse and worked the land, according to the 1851 census.

Robert Moss who owned 375 acres, was the only major landowner to live in the village, at the Manor House, now demolished and the site of New Manor residential home. He owned nine farms, three smallholdings, a house and three cottages and his main tenant was William Breakell whose farm was situated off Brownhill Lane.

A number of smaller landowners had also seen their opportunity and bought land as it came available. Some were from old-established local families such as the Parks. Robert Park owned Grove Cottage and the adjoining land (now The Coppice) while John Park lived and worked Park Farm on Marsh Lane. Others, however, had made their money in business and had bought land and property with the proceeds. John Taylor, a druggist, owned three farms, a house and garden at Pilot Cottage on Grange Lane, and two other cottages. Similarly, another John Taylor, a seedsman, had a farm and land at New Longton and a plantation off Back Lane. Lawrence Rawstorne of Penwortham Priory, and 'impropriator' of the tithes of the parish, had bought sixteen acres in New Longton, while John Brown, who owned the Farmers' Arms at Whitestake with 100 acres attached, also had a house and five cottages leased to local tenants. I have referred previously to Garstang and Clarkson, cheese factors, who had consistently invested in cottage property in the area (see Chapter Three).

In 1838, it was estimated that there were some 678 acres of arable land, 1,750 acres of meadow or pasture, 119 acres of barren waste or uncultivated land, and 146 acres of marsh adjoining the rivers Ribble and Asland (Douglas), liable for payment of tithe. There were also 357 acres occupied by houses and cottages and their attached gardens, on which, of course, tithe also had to be paid. The annual rent charge which was required in lieu of tithe after the Tithe Commutation Act was calculated on the price of corn, wheat, barley and oats per bushel, and this gave lay 'impropriator' Lawrence Rawstorne £338 per year, and the curate of Penwortham £8 in respect of the 'Small Tithes, Dues, Easter Offerings and Mortuaries'.

The Tithe Schedule of 1838 provides details of the crops which were grown in the fields on the accompanying map. There were just over 100 acres of wheat, 185 acres of oats and some 75 acres devoted to growing potatoes. Most of the wheat was grown on the drained land at New Longton, in the area bounded by Gill Lane, Sod Hall Lane, Wham Lane and Drumacre Lane, and in the fields at the lower end of Hall Carr Lane and Marsh Lane. Oats were grown in fields to the southeast of New Longton and off Hall Carr Lane adjoining Longton Marsh, but also in several fields to the north of Chapel Lane. Potatoes were grown in the above areas and quite a number of 'moss pieces' in New Longton were also given over to their cultivation.

Efforts were being made to improve the land, for there were 85 acres of clover, 7 acres of vetches and 5 of beans. Such crops, which were sown in the autumn, provided green manure by fixing nitrogen in the soil which was gradually released in the spring. But this was only on a small scale, and not to the extent which Lawrence Rawstorne envisaged. There were about 950 acres of meadowland which provided hay for animal fodder, and some 800 acres of pasture. It is therefore apparent that local farmers concentrated primarily on cattle and fodder crops and in supplying the growing demand for dairy produce. In Longton, the acreage of arable land was only 20% of the total of 3,383 acres, whereas 55% consisted of meadow and pasture. In surrounding parishes such as Burscough, Rufford, Tarleton, Bickerstaffe, Ormskirk and Scarisbrick, some 47% of land use was devoted to arable and pasture in 1849.[78]

Local farms were small compared with England as a whole. In 1838 only two farms were over one hundred acres: fourteen had acreages between one hundred and fifty, twenty-nine farms were between fifty and twenty acres, and thirty-seven below twenty acres. Most farmers relied principally upon their own families to work the land, and in many cases these were little more than smallholdings, providing a pretty basic existence. There could have been little profit when a thirteen-acre farm, for example, supported a widower, four unmarried sons and a daughter. Several single women tenanted local farms, relying upon brothers, sisters-in-law and nephews to work on the land in return for providing them with a home.

Nationally, agriculture accounted for about a quarter of all male employment at this time.[79] In Longton in 1851, 48% of men worked on the land. Over half of these were tenant farmers and farmers' sons, and the rest farm servants and agricultural labourers. Farm servants lived in with their employer, whereas the labourer had his own small cottage nearby. A third class of migrant workers, frequently handloom weavers, sought work on the larger farms at haymaking time, but these are not revealed in the census, which was made in November 1851, well after haymaking was over.

Farming and weaving had been inextricably linked for many years, but in most cases, holdings were very small, usually under five acres. Others combined farming with business interests, like James Lathom who had three acres on Hall Carr Lane and also ran a grocer's shop. Most of the innkeepers owned adjacent farm-land, like John Brown with one hundred acres near the Farmer's Arms, John Taylor at the Black Bull with twenty acres and William Whittle with twenty-two acres at the Red Lion. It was in these latter cases that farm servants were employed, and they were single men, some born locally or from neighbouring townships like Bretherton and Leyland. There were only sixteen farm servants listed in the 1851 census.

Farming in Longton had had its problems in the 1820s. Farm prices had risen sharply as a consequence of the blockade of British shipping during the Napoleonic Wars, but after peace was signed in 1815, a period of uncertainty set in. Agriculture was in a depressed state in the country areas around Preston in 1821–22, and in 1820, the Longton villagers had each been given fifteen loads of coal and half an ox to eke out their own meagre supplies.[80]

By the 1850s conditions had improved marginally, but local people showed a stubborn conservatism in respect of any change in their way of life. The improvement in transport following the the establishment of the turnpike roads had provided some economic stimulus, and helped to reduce the differential between town and country wages.

Some of the younger people had left the village, lured by the hope of higher wages, the chance of earlier marriage and more social amusements in Preston. But many labourers, with a cottage and a small garden attached to it, were loath to exchange this for a tenement and work in a factory. People in their forties and upwards weighed up the pros and cons, and decided to stay where they were. They had their farms, albeit small, and a little extra from weaving, and hoped for better times.

Nationally, however, times did not improve for those engaged in agriculture. A series of bad harvests, cheap grain imports from North America, Russia and India, together with refrigerated meat from Australia and America, had serious repercussions. In 1851, agriculture had employed one in six of the male workforce, but by 1881, this was reduced to one in ten.

Yet Longton men continued to rely heavily upon farming and ancillary trades for their livelihood, as the 1881 census shows. 37% of all men and boys were farmers, farmers' sons or farm labourers. The number of farm servants 'living in' had, however, doubled since 1851, although they continued to be young single men employed on the largest farms. This was probably due in part to the greater affluence of the larger tenant farmers who could afford to employ farm servants, and to the end of the casual labour which handloom weaving had provided. There was also a group of eight migrant agricultural workers, four of whom were Irish, and the others from as far afield as Scotland, Stafford and Shropshire. In 1881, they all lodged with Edward Walsh (seventy) and his wife on School Lane. Edward, a hawker selling articles door-to-door, had been born in Ballylongford in Ireland, and hence the connection with the four Irish labourers, one of whose wives provided their meals. The influx of Irish labourers had begun in 1845 after the failure of the potato crop, which created famine and the consequent emigration of nearly a million people, mainly to America, but also to the British mainland. The subsequent poverty of the Irish economy meant that many men left their smallholdings in the charge of their wives and spent several months each year in England, often moving from one area to another for the hay harvest, the corn harvest and later for lifting potatoes. Living together and eating frugally, they could, even allowing for travelling expenses, make between £13 10s. and £17 to take back home at the end of the season.

By 1881, the size of farm holdings in Longton had changed. Whereas in England as a whole there was a trend towards larger farms which could be managed more economically making use of mechanised equipment, and in consequence, reducing the number of labourers required, in Longton the trend was towards smaller holdings. Compared with 1851, there were thirty farms between fifty and twenty acres, forty-one between twenty and five acres and fifteen smallholdings of less than five acres, and an increase of only one farm of over one hundred acres. Many of the 1851 tenants had been replaced by newcomers, although younger members of some of the old families remained.

There is little evidence of the extent to which women were involved in agricultural work. However, in 1856 Nathaniel

Hawthorne[81] noted that near Southport 'people were harvesting their carrots and other root crops and women as well as men were at work, especially digging potatoes', and in 1871 at Rufford, women were 'planting potatoes and spreading dung'.[82] Most Longton farmers' wives and daughters must have helped on the family farm and were accustomed to heavy manual work when necessary.

Lancashire's agricultural workers had always been better paid than elsewhere in rural England. In 1850–51 for example, agricultural wages in Lancashire averaged 13*s.* 6*d* per week compared with 7*s.* 0*d* in Suffolk. By the 1890s an average agricultural wage in West Lancashire had risen to 19*s.* 0*d* per week, compared with 15*s.* 0*d* in Norfolk.[83] This was largely due to the availability of alternative employment. The prodigious growth of industrial towns like Preston, Manchester and Liverpool created a comparable increase in demand for foodstuffs and farm produce. But Longton, at least until the coming of the railway in 1882, was not ideally placed to take advantage. People still disposed of their farm produce and brought in their supplies in a variety of ways.

The proximity of the River Douglas had its advantages. A document dated 1797[84] refers to the loading and unloading of goods from coastal vessels which plied along the west coast mainly from Liverpool, goods such as 'Oats, Wheat, Barley, Malt, Potatoes – Slate, Stones, Timber, Coal, Canel, Goods and Merchandizes'. A charge was levied on all goods loaded and unloaded, and paid to the inspector appointed by the owners of cattle 'gates' on Longton Marsh. This preserved the grazing rights of the 'gate' owners, but allowed 'such Person and Persons as are Inhabitants of Longton – actually residing there' to load and unload coal and cannell for their own use free of charge. But how long this trade continued is not known. Pilot Cottage at the far end of Grange Lane is indicative of the fact that a pilot was necessary to guide vessels through the hazardous shifting sands and marshland which had created a problem for river navigation for centuries. However, in 1851, a weaver lived at Pilot Cottage and there is no mention of a pilot in the census.

The potential of the River Douglas became apparent with the demand for coal from the Wigan coalfield, which was hampered by having to rely on transport by road.[85] An outlet on the south bank of the Ribble would open up trade with the Fylde coast and help offset the problem of the shallow draft of the Ribble between Lytham and Preston. In 1720, work began to make the Douglas navigable between Wigan and its confluence with the River Ribble, but progress was slow due to lack of finance. By 1742, however, the work was basically completed, comprising thirteen locks, although later a new section of canal had to be built between Sollom and Rufford, subsequently extended to Tarleton. Coal, cannel, turf and paving stones were the principal commodities carried downstream, with limestone, timber, hides, soap ash and barley comprising the main return cargoes.

Transport of goods by road remained difficult, despite the building of the Preston to Liverpool turnpike in 1771. The road surface between Tarleton and Preston was indifferent, and local people had to leave Tarleton as early as 2 a.m. to reach Preston market in time for its opening at 5 a.m.[86] Routes across country were still almost impassable at certain times of the year because of the marshy terrain. At Bretherton 'the waters of the Lostock frequently rise, so as to cut off the whole population from the opportunity of uniting with their neighbours in the public worship of Almighty God',[87] and conditions were no better to the south around Crossens and Banks. Farm produce such as milk and cheese could only have been carried short distances in the days before refrigeration. For Longton farmers, Preston must have been their preferred market, using the turnpike road and the old bridge across the Ribble at Penwortham.

Lancashire had pioneered the railway age with the opening of the Liverpool to Manchester line in 1830. West Lancashire farmers quickly saw the benefits of investing in the Liverpool, Crosby and Southport line of 1848, taking 'as many five pound shares as they could spare the money of'.[88] The opening of a station in 1868 at Midge Hall as part of the Preston–Liverpool line undoubtedly encouraged the growth of market-gardening in the New Longton area. Yet Longton remained isolated until 1882, when a group of Methodist worthies in Southport promoted the building of the West Lancashire Railway. Laudable as their motives were, and certainly the line enabled Longton farmers to dispose of their produce and local traders to buy a greater variety of goods to sell locally, the line was a financial white elephant. 'With little traffic in this out of the way corner of Lancashire, the West Lancashire Railway was a poverty-stricken concern which never paid a dividend and was unable to keep up its debenture payments'[89] and was incorporated into the Lancashire and Yorkshire Railway in 1897. Nevertheless, Longton had arrived on the railway map, and even by the census of 1881 the benefits were anticipated in the increase in the number of general dealers, dealers specialising in hay, straw and potatoes and farm fertilisers, as well as carters and carriers, as we shall see later.

Even in 1881, railway construction was still a very labour-intensive undertaking. Steam navvies were first used in 1850 to excavate rock and difficult terrain but the West Lancashire Railway, impoverished as it was, even with flat countryside with few natural obstacles, relied almost entirely on manual labour recruited locally or from the considerable army of 'navvies' who moved from site to site (we saw who they were in Chapter Eight). Their work was with pick and shovel, cutting out the track bed, laying pipes and rubble drains, plate-laying and trimming and spreading topsoil on the embankments. The permanent way was constructed of coarse gravel on which the sleepers were laid and drilled to take the chairs which held the steel rails, each secured by a key and fish-plated together. The track had then to be aligned and packed

New Longton Station, Chapel Lane. The station was opened in 1882.

with ballast. Although the bridges were built of stone, the station at Longton Bridge was constructed of brick with a slate roof. The 1911 OS map clearly shows the layout, built on the site of the old workhouse. There were platforms on either side of the double line, a passenger station building, a goods yard with cattle pens, a weighbridge and a warehouse on the School Lane side. There was a signal box across the tracks and later two lines forming a narrow gauge tramway leading to the brickworks, which were established at the turn of the century. The station at New Longton was originally called Howick but was renamed Hutton and Howick in 1897 by the Lancashire and Yorkshire Railway, and subsequently called New Longton only in 1934. It was not until 1911 that Penwortham Cop Lane Station was opened. Despite its rather poverty-stricken beginnings, the line provided not only a valuable suburban passenger service, but a freight service for farmers and the growing community until its closure under the Beeching Act in 1964.

The opening of the station in 1882 must have been a major event in the village. That summer, the Sunday School teachers' trip from St Mary's, Penwortham, to Southport[90] 'employed this year the first Railway Train that ever took up passengers in the Township of Penwortham ... The day was very fine and greatly enjoyed, and both the Company and the Contractors (Braddock and Matthews) did everything for the convenience and safety of the travellers'. This contrasts with a previous Sunday School trip made to Southport in 1875, via Burscough Junction. 'Train starts from Preston at 7.00 a.m. We are sorry that the Railway company (L and Y.R.) have refused to make any reduction on the regular fares – a very shabby act of the Company. The fare will therefore be 2s.9d'.

The coming of the railway age had not met with universal approval at national level. The Duke of Wellington had declared 'I see no reason to suppose that these machines will ever force themselves into general use.' In 1844, William Wordsworth had written to Mr Gladstone about the proposed line from Kendal to Windermere: 'the project if carried into effect will destroy the staple of the County which is its beauty, and on the Lord's Day particularly, will prove subversive of its quiet, and be highly injurious to its morals.' The sense of outrage about Sunday travel was considerable and Trollope's Mrs Proudie was incensed. Even in 1889, the Anti-Sunday Travel Union boasted fifty-eight branches and 8,000 members,[91] and partly because of its lobbying, suburban trains were excluded from timetables during the hours of church services. Timetables themselves used Greenwich or London time, but local time differed and converting early timetables to meet local station services was highly inconvenient, until 'Railway Time' was accepted everywhere in Britain by 1852.

As with time, so in many other ways railways gave some uniformity to the countryside. Areas originally remote could now be visited. Early opposition faded on the face of the benefits which the railways brought. The local station provided a link with the outside world. Those few towns which rejected the railway mania declined and subsequently decayed. To most people, the railways were the epitome of the Victorian age, providing freedom to see new sights, meet new people from all walks of life, and above all to benefit from the speedy transportation of goods of all sorts. Villages no longer needed to be self-sufficient: indeed to have no station was to be excluded from civilisation. People marvelled at the ingenuity of the railway engineers and the scale of their achievements.

To Longton people, the opening of the station in 1882 enabled them to travel further afield to work and to take a trip to more distant places. Farmers could sell their produce in wider markets and shopkeepers introduce new and more varied goods for sale. But not everyone could afford to use the train. An old Longton resident, remembering his childhood, said 'Furthest we ever got

Longton Bridge Station shows the platform for Preston Trains, with ticket and staff offices and waiting room. Gas lamps and the signal box can be seen on the right. The station was closed by Dr Beeching in 1964.

was Longton Marsh, we never got to Southport'. For many, those first trips by train engendered anticipation and excitement, which was in some cases too much to endure: 'People who find it necessary to vomit while in a railway carriage should discreetly use their hats; this would come naturally to anyone properly brought up'.[92] Despite this, the distinction of first, second and third class compartments, waiting and dining rooms and the smell of smoke and the soot from the engine, travelling by train remained an adventure in the nineteenth century.

CHAPTER ELEVEN

The End of the Victorian Age

HE CENSUS of 1901 shows, for the first time in eighty years, an increase rather than a decrease in Longton's population. From 1891, when the total was 1,333, virtually what it had been in 1811, it reached 1,707 in 1901. Little and Much Hoole and Howick had a similar population pattern at this time, although Hutton, even by 1901, had not regained its figure of 1811. Penwortham and Farington were completely different. Penwortham saw a steady increase from 1801 until by 1901 it had doubled in size, already becoming a commuter area for Preston. Farington, however, from a population of 382 in 1801, had reached 2,005 a hundred years later, reflecting the influx into the local textile factories.

By 1900 the impact of improved living standards, greater accessibility to goods and services provided by the local railway station and more varied job opportunities for both men and women, had imperceptibly changed Longton from a rural back-water to a more outgoing and prosperous community.

Trade directories issued between 1900 and 1913 show an increase in tradesmen, particularly in bricklayers, joiners, painters and general building contractors, and shopkeepers, including grocers, butchers, fishmongers and tailors. Even a watchmaker and cycle dealer had set up business, the latter to cater for the increase in

Longton Brickcroft, North lake. The water-filled pit was left by the clay extractions to produce bricks from 1897 until the 1950s. The company who owned the site ceased production in the 1960s, and the site remained derelict for twenty years until 1987 when South Ribble council acquired the land. The site is now a nature reserve and conservation area.

cycling, especially among cycling clubs, before the coming of the first motor cars. The village at long last had its own doctor's surgery, and local branches of the London, City and Midland Bank and the Manchester and Liverpool District Banking Company had opened. Bricks and tiles were manufactured on the site near the station – now Longton Brickcroft – and the Wilkins Brewery on Marsh Lane was a flourishing concern.

When, on New Year's Eve, villagers gathered in their homes or in the local public houses to toast the advent of the twentieth century, they probably looked forward confidently to the future.

Yet on 22 January 1901 Queen Victoria died. The end of the Victorian age and the dawn of the new century gave many pause for thought, to evaluate past achievements and to wonder what the future would hold. If they read the national press – and by 1901 97% of men and 96% of women were literate – it was clear that all was not well.

Although London remained the world's financial centre the country's economic supremacy was challenged by strong foreign competition, and relations with the rest of Europe were uneasy. Although Britain had, between 1886 and 1899, successfully divided up most of the African continent with Germany, France, Italy and Portugal without going to war, the situation in South Africa was more intractable. The Boers in the Orange Free State and the Transvaal were increasingly resentful of British policy in neighbouring Natal and the Cape Colony, and aided by arms imported from Germany in 1899 they invaded and inflicted humiliation on the British troops at Ladysmith, Mafeking and Kimberley. The war dragged on until 1902, but involving as it did forces from Australia, New Zealand and Canada, it was a portent of the scale of future political conflicts.

The Boer War revealed not only Britain's military and technical unpreparedness for large-scale conflict, but also the poor physical condition of over a quarter of the men who volunteered for active service from such towns as York, Sheffield and Leeds and who were rejected as unfit on medical grounds.

These figures brought into sharp focus the continuing gulf between the rich and the poor. Although general living standards had improved, Edwardian social reformers, unlike their Victorian predecessors, were now concerned with issues of social justice and the unequal distribution of the nation's wealth. People's expectations of what constituted a decent, tolerable and fair standard of living had risen above mere survival, through the efforts of such reformers as Seebohm Rowntree, Sir Charles Booth and Beatrice Webb. Demands grew for increased government intervention to bring about better wages and working conditions, improved urban housing, old age pensions and better health care, to improve the lot of the working classes.[93]

These demands came from radical elements in political society. Between 1874 and 1906, government swung between the party system with the Conservatives, dominated by Disraeli, Lord Salisbury and Balfour on the one hand, and the Liberals with Gladstone and Lord Rosebury on the other.[94] In 1886, half the members of Parliament came from the aristocracy and landed classes, although by 1900 their members had declined to less than a third of the total number of MPs. Both political parties were largely dominated by *laissez faire* policies and neither wished to alienate their traditional support by embarking on radical social change.

Gradually the right to vote was extended. By 1884, about five million adult males over the age of twenty-one were entitled to vote – some 28% of the adult population – and a secret ballot had been introduced in 1872. The movement for the right of women to vote had begun in 1867, but achieved little success. After the formation of the Sufragettes in 1903, the campaign became more militant, but it was not until the Reform Act of 1918, when all adult males became entitled to the vote, that Parliament extended the franchise to women over thirty, largely in recognition of their contribution to the war effort in 1914–18. It was only in 1928 that all women became eligible to vote.

Meanwhile trade unionism developed rapidly from 1889, although socialism among such groups as the Fabian Society grew more slowly than in the rest of Europe. Nevertheless, by 1893 the Independent Labour Party was founded, drawing its support from voters newly enfranchised in 1884, who, disaffected with Liberal policies, responded to the demand for social equality and the traditional working-class desire for self-education.

Yet these challenges to the existing political establishment were still in their infancy, and the Edwardian years were ones of political uncertainty and only limited social legislation.

If the political scene was one of doubt, pressure for social reform was increasing. Edward VII's reign was a time of pleasure-seeking and a relaxation of the Victorian attitude to morality and social rectitude. The king surrounded himself with a circle of aristocratic friends and enjoyed an almost endless round of pleasurable activities which encompassed a succession of female companions. This inevitably brought women's role in society into sharp focus. Bernard Shaw's *Mrs Warren's Profession* brought prostitution not only into the theatre but into public debate. The Victorian ideal of the woman as the bastion of marriage and domestic values, totally subservient to man, was losing force, as more and more women were writing, going out into society unchaperoned and above all, taking advantage of increasing employment opportunities.

Meanwhile, at the opposite end of the social scale, the working class of both sexes had more basic concerns. The ever-present fear of unemployment was paramount, even among skilled workers. The problems of feeding the family, inability to pay the rent, loss of status and dread of illness, debility and industrial accident, were major concerns for the working class.

Although the nation's state of health had improved by 1900, it was certainly not up to today's standard. The Boer War recruitment figures had been a sober reminder that the health of the lower classes was a matter for serious concern. Most of them were unable to afford qualified medical advice and relied instead on patent and herbal remedies.

Lack of ante-natal care, and to some extent Victorian prudery, meant that most women had a very real fear of childbirth and knew little of contraceptive methods. Old age was also an anxiety if one could no longer live at home or be cared for by relatives. The shadow of the workhouse was never far away. Intended as a deterrent to the idle, and a means of coping with the sick and mentally ill, it was totally inappropriate for the care of the elderly and frail.

The influence of the social reformers and their enquiries into the effects of unemployment, old age and poverty, revealed that charity and philanthropy were no longer adequate to cope. The middle-class attitude that the social conditions of the poor were largely caused by fecklessness and lack of motivation also began to change.

Gradually, therefore, Government was forced to accept that state intervention was necessary to tackle the 'condition of the people', as it came to be regarded. The way in which this was to be achieved was a new phenomenon. Faced with the entrenched attitudes of private and vested interests, the lack of knowledge on how to proceed, and above all the cost of its administration, the government was entering totally new territory. Even more fundamental to the 'condition of the people' was the question of how much the state should intervene to provide a good life for the majority, and indeed, what constituted a good life. The declining influence of organised religion and the doubts created by scientific discoveries led many to question their own beliefs, which now seemed simplistic. Religion had taught that belief in God would enable one to lead a 'good life', but if that belief had gone, then what was the basis of everyday life?

These factors contributed to the government's uncertain response.

The Education Acts passed between 1867 and 1902 were largely piecemeal and did nothing to reduce social divisions. The state primary and secondary schools catered for working-class children and gave them basic instruction in the three 'R's, a smattering of history, geography and religious teaching, with sewing for girls and woodwork for boys. The great public schools and the better private schools continued to provide an education which led to careers in the professions and the perpetuation of class elitism. In 1908, an Old Age Pensions Act was passed, and the 1911 Health Act enabled the poor to to be accepted by the panel of doctors who were prepared to take part in the scheme.

The establishment of county councils in 1888, and district and parish councils in 1894, gradually replaced the old multiplicity of local officials whose powers had often overlapped one another. But the relationship between central government and local authorities brought with it central control through increased bureaucracy, and an ever-escalating requirement for grants to enable services to be provided at local level. Certainly progress had been made, despite the reluctance of government to accept that financial help from the state was not an abandonment of the moral principle of self-help. Despite electoral reforms, the public at large was indifferent and ill-informed. The real problem was how to pay

Numbers 57 and 59 Chapel Lane, originally the Primitive Methodist Chapel built in 1837.

Liverpool Road, present day.

for the radical reforms which were essential, and the answer lay in a new attitude to taxation. Lloyd George's budget of 1909 was introduced for 'raising money to wage implacable warfare against poverty and squalidness', and recommended rates of standard and 'super tax' on income. But the House of Lords, which personified vested interest and upper class wealth, voted the budget out and created thereby a constitutional turning point. From then onwards they lost the constitutional power to exert control over financial bills. By the outbreak of war in 1914, taxation became inevitable and accepted as a fact of life. This precedent was to be a vital factor in the future establishment of the Welfare State.

Looking back over the later years of the nineteenth century, although much had been achieved, much remained to be done. Perhaps the greatest achievement was the gradual realisation that the social injustice of the gulf between the rich and the poor must be addressed, and that ordinary men and women had a right to a secure future with acceptable housing and working conditions. But the sense of unease remained.

The catalyst which focused this unease was the outbreak of the Great War in 1914. The development of the popular press, with its ever-simplified sensationalism, fuelled the national need to find a cause for the country's ills. Germany, with its imperial and industrial challenge, was regarded as the cause.

Consequently the declaration of war in August was greeted with great patriotic fervour and a confidence that it would all be over by Christmas. When the lists of dead and wounded began to be published, however, Britain quickly realised that this war was like no other before it. By 1918 nobody was in any doubt that the country would never be the same again. Britain had led the world into the industrial age with its technology and had reaped its reward in the attendant prosperity and confidence it had created. But the Edwardian years and the Great War had shattered all that. On New Year's Eve, 1900, Longton toasted the new century unaware, unlike the historian, of what lay ahead.

References

1. Eve McLaughlin, *The Censuses, 1841–1881: Use and Interpretation* (F.F.H.S., 1979).

2. R. Lawton (ed.), *The Census and Social Structure* (Frank Cass, 1978).

3. D.V. Glass, *Numbering the People* (Saxon House, 1972).

4. Bagley and Hodgkiss, *Lancashire: A History of the County Palatine in Early Maps* (Neil Richardson, 1985).

5. R. Porter, *English Society in the Eighteenth Century* (Pelican, 1982).

6. *Ibid.*

7. *Ibid.*

8. Blackstone, *Commentaries on the Laws of England.*

9. W.W. Roscoe, *Stages of Economic Growth* (Cambridge, 1960).

10. James Kay Shuttleworth.

11. J.F.C. Harrison, *Early Victorian Britain, 1832–1851* (Fontana, 1979).

12. *Ibid.*

13. J. L. and B. Hammond, *The Town Labourer and the Industrial Revolution.*

14. D. Marshall, *Industrial England 1776–1851* (Routledge & Kegan Paul, 1973).

15. J. K. Walton, *Lancashire: A Social History, 1558–1939* (Manchester University Press, 1987).

16. *Ibid.*

17. P.J. Gooderson, *A History of Lancashire* (Batsford, 1980).

18. A. Crosby, *Penwortham in the Past* (Carnegie Publishing, 1988).

19. M. Anderson, *Family Structure in Nineteenth-Century Lancashire* (Cambridge University Press, 1974).

20. J. D. Marshall, *The Lancashire Rural Labourer in the Early Nineteenth Century*, Lancashire and Cheshire Antiquarian Society, vol. 71 (1961).

21. Anderson, *op. cit.*

22. J.F.C. Harrison, *op. cit.*

23. C. Gardner, 'The Care of the Sick Poor of Preston in the Nineteenth Century', thesis 1957.

24. S. Peter Bell (ed.), *Victorian Lancashire* (David & Charles, 1974).

25. J.F.C. Harrison, *op. cit.*

26. E. C. Midwinter, *Social Administration in Lancashire, 1830–60* (Manchester University Press, 1969).

27. F. Engels. *The Condition of the Working Class in England* (1844).

28. Dutton and King, *Ten Percent and No Surrender* (Cambridge University Press, 1981).

29. N. Longmate, *The Hungry Mills: the story of the Lancashire Cotton Famine 1861/5* (Temple Smith, 1978).

30. P. Fleetwood Hesketh, *Lancashire Architectural Guide* (J. Murray, 1955).

31. Bell (ed.), *op. cit.*

32. G. E. Mingay, *Rural Life in Victorian England* (Heinemann, 1977).

33. P. Horn, *The Victorian Country Child* (Alan Sutton, 1985).

34. A. Hewitson, *Our Country Churches and Chapels* (1872).

35. *Ibid.*

36. LRO, DDHe 83/54.

37. Hewitson, *op. cit.*

38. Crosby, *op. cit.*

39. A. Rogers, *This Was Their World* (BBC, 1972).

40. *Marriage and Divorce Statistics 1837–1983* (HMSO)

41. Rogers, *op. cit.*

42. F. M. L. Thompson, *The Rise of Respectable Society* (Fontana, 1988).

43. Crosby, *op. cit.*

44. LRO, DDHe 83/57, 83/61.

45. LRO, PR 2381.

46. P. Horn, *Labouring Life in the Victorian Countryside* (Alan Sutton, 1976).

47. R. Dobson, *Policing in Lancashire 1839–1989* (Landy Publishing, 1989).

48. P. Horn, *The Rise and Fall of the Victorian Servant* (Gill & Macmillan, 1975).

49. Barker and Drake (eds), *Population and Society in Britain, 1850–1980* (Batsford, 1982).

50. Wadsworth and Mann, *The Cotton Trade and Industrial Lancashire 1660–1780* (Manchester University Press, 1931).

51. S. Sartin, *The People and Places of Historic Preston* (Carnegie Publishing, 1988).

52. G. Timmins, *The Last Shift: the decline of the handloom* (Manchester University Press, 1993).

53. *Ibid.*

54. LRO, DDHs ledgers A–J.

55. LRO, Cost Book DDHs 75.

56. Timmins, *op. cit.*

57. S. Peters (ed.), *Victorian Lancashire* (David & Charles, 1974).

58. Timmins, *op. cit.*

59. D. Bythill, *The Handloom Weavers* (Cambridge University Press, 1969).

60. Holt, *A General View of Agriculture in the County of Lancaster* (1795).

61. A. Hodge, *History of Preston: An Introduction* (Carnegie Publishing, 1984).

62. P. Horn, *Labouring Life in the Victorian Countryside* (Alan Sutton, 1987).

63. F.M.L. Thompson, *op. cit.*

64. D. Brooke, *The Railway Navvy* (David & Charles, 1983).

65. Lawton (ed.), *op. cit.*

66. P. Horn, *op. cit.*

67. G. Best, *Mid-Victorian Britain, 1851–75* (Fontana, 1979).

68. F.M.L. Thompson, *op. cit.*

69. *Ibid.*

70. P. Horn. *op. cit.*

71. *Ibid.*

72. Hewitson, *op. cit.*

73. Charity Commission Report, Parish of Penwortham (HMSO, 1901).

74. *St Andrew's Church: a short guide* (1959).

75. Charity Commission report, *op. cit.*

76. J. Barnett (ed.), *Destiny Obscure: Autobiographies of Childhood, Education and Family 1820–1920* (Allen Lane, 1982).

77. 'Serious Manures, some comparisons between Flanders and Lancashire 1790–1860', in A. Crosby (ed.), *Lancashire Local Studies* (Carnegie Publishing, 1993).

78. A. Mutch, *Rural Life in South West Lancashire 1840–1914* (Centre for North-West Regional Studies, University of Lancaster).

79. P. Horn, *op. cit.*

80. J.D. Marshall, *The Lancashire Rural Labourer in the Early Nineteenth Century*, Lancashire and Cheshire Antiquarian Society, vol. 71 (1961).

81. N. Hawthorne, *The English Notebooks* (New York, 1941).

82. A. Mutch, *op. cit.*

83. *Ibid.*

84. LRO, DDLa 7/18.

85. M. Clarke, *The Leeds & Liverpool Canal: A History and Guide* (Carnegie Publishing, 1990).

86. J. Cotterall, *North Meols to South Ribble* (N. Richarson, 1985).

87. A. Mutch, *op. cit.*

88. G. Holt, *The Regional History of the Railways, vol. 10, The North West.*

89. *Ibid.*

90. St Mary's, Penwortham, parish magazine, No. 9.

91. M. Robbins, *The Railway Age* (Routledge & Kegan Paul, 1962).

92. Stuart Legg (ed.), *The Railway Book* (Hart Davis, 1952).

93. J. Roebuck, *The Making of Modern English Society from 1850* (Routledge & Kegan Paul, 1973).

94. J. F. C. Harrison, *op. cit.*

Other town and city histories available from Carnegie:

Prof. John K. Walton, *Blackpool*

Peter Aughton, *Bristol: A People's History*

Dr John A. Hargreaves, *Halifax*

Dr Andrew White (ed.), *A History of Lancaster*

Peter Aughton, *Liverpool: A People's History*

Prof. Alan Kidd, *Manchester*

Dr Jeffrey Hill, *Nelson*

Prof. David Hey, *A History of Sheffield*

Forthcoming town and city histories:

Dr Graham Davis and Penny Bonsall, *A History of Bath*

Prof. Carl Chinn, *Birmingham*

Dr Derek Beattie, *Blackburn*

Dr John Doran, *Chester*

Dr John A. Hargreaves, *Huddersfield*

Prof. Trevor Rowley, *A History of Oxford*

Dr Mark Freeman, *A History of St Albans*

Dr John B. Smith, *Wolverhampton*

Prof. Bill Sheils, *A History of York*

Full details on **www.carnegiepublishing.com**